AS UNIONS MATURE

A PROJECT OF THE
INDUSTRIAL RELATIONS SECTION
PRINCETON UNIVERSITY

As Unions Mature

An Analysis of the Evolution of American Unionism

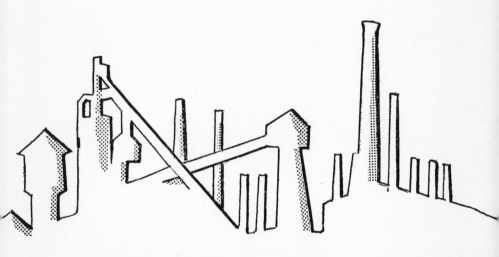

BY RICHARD A. LESTER

PRINCETON, NEW JERSEY

PRINCETON UNIVERSITY PRESS

1958

□□□□□□□□□□□□□□□□□□□□□□□□□□□□□□

FOREWORD

WITHIN the past decades a number of excellent books have been written about American labor unions. Some have analyzed why workers join unions and what they think is the appropriate role of unions in representing their interests. Others have stressed collective relations with employers, and a few have traced the history of individual labor organizations. As a result, there is now quite an impressive body of authoritative knowledge concerning the function and structure of labor organizations, the processes of collective bargaining, the personal histories of particular labor leaders, and the people who make up the ranks of the union. The extensive attention given to unions in the literature of our time is a reflection of their vital importance in modern American society.

Yet, comparatively little attention has been given to the evolution and the growth processes of unions. It is apparent that the well-established and relatively powerful labor organizations of today think and act differently than they did twenty-five years ago. The problems confronting the newly organized unions which were struggling in the thirties to establish beachheads in industries long characterized by hostility to organized labor are not the same as those faced today by strong, stable, and secure labor organizations. Unions as well as other economic and political institutions have undergone great changes over the years.

In this volume, Professor Lester has highlighted a very important emerging problem area in industrial relations— the effect of the maturing process on the vitality and responsiveness of labor organizations. He has traced the direc-

[v]

tions in which organized labor has been growing, and he has provided significant new insights into the issues of public policy which come to the fore as unions reach institutional middle age. An interpretive "think-piece" of this kind, coming from an economist with a distinguished reputation of long-standing in the labor field, should greatly increase understanding and perception in industrial relations. It makes an important contribution toward the development of a theory of union behavior.

This study is a research publication of the Industrial Relations Section at Princeton. As part of the Department of Economics and Sociology, the Section conducts a program of teaching and research in industrial relations and the related field of economic development, and sponsors conferences and seminars for practitioners in industry and labor unions. The major research areas of the Section are: (1) The comparative study of labor problems in industrialized and undeveloped countries abroad; (2) the industrial relations problems encountered by American corporations operating in foreign countries; (3) manpower utilization problems as related to industrial growth in the United States; and (4) the orientation and problems of mature unionism. In all of these areas, the Section has sought to concern itself with the development of insights, the interpretation of concepts, and the analysis of questions of national and international policy. This volume represents the completion of several years of work in the last area.

FREDERICK H. HARBISON
DIRECTOR, INDUSTRIAL RELATIONS SECTION
PRINCETON UNIVERSITY

PREFACE

AMERICANS often react emotionally toward labor unions. Instead of passing judgment, this book examines the directions in which organized labor has been moving in this country and weighs the implications of union evolution.

As a pioneer attempt in an emotionally-charged area, this little volume is bound to provoke disagreement and controversy. At the outset it should be made clear that I am explaining, not what I should like to see happen but what appear to me to have been the main developments and what they seem to signify. When such words as "evolution" and "maturity" are used, it should be emphasized that they carry no necessary implication of progress, virtue, or social advantage.

Certainly the writer of such a book as this cannot expect agreement with every assumption and conclusion. My efforts will be sufficiently rewarded if this analysis provokes other interpretations or even union actions that raise doubts concerning some of my main propositions.

Since this book has had a long period of gestation, many persons have, in one way or another, contributed to its development. One important influence has been the discussions in the Trade Union Seminars at Princeton. I recall particularly the sessions led by Arthur Schlesinger, Jr. in 1953 and by Daniel Bell in 1954, in which the union participants presented sharply dissenting positions. Valuable criticism was received when some of the ideas in this book were presented before the Graduate Economics Seminar at Massachusetts Institute of Technology in April 1957.

[vii]

PREFACE

Helpful suggestions and criticisms of the first draft of the manuscript were received from Herbert S. Bailey, Jr. of the Princeton University Press; William G. Bowen of Princeton University; George W. Brooks of the International Brotherhood of Pulp, Sulphite, and Paper Mill Workers; David L. Cole, arbitrator and former Director of the Federal Mediation and Conciliation Service; Frederick H. Harbison of the Industrial Relations Section; and Dale Yoder of the Industrial Relations Center of the University of Minnesota. However, I alone bear responsibility for the final product.

I am indebted to the Industrial Relations Section of Princeton University for financial and other support while this book was in preparation. Princeton University provided a sabbatical leave so that I could spend half a year investigating trade unionism in Europe, especially in Britain and Sweden.

R.A.L.

Princeton, N.J.
November 20, 1957

CONTENTS

[ix]

CONTENTS

CONTENTS

AS UNIONS MATURE

I. INTRODUCTION

TRADE UNIONISM IN AMERICA has come of age. Some 18 million workers are enrolled in its ranks. The power and influence of unions penetrate not only the workplace but also the financial centers, the community chest, and even foreign aid. It may be idle to argue whether we have arrived at a "laboristic society"—the term Sumner Slichter applies to a community in which an employee viewpoint predominates. But, obviously, labor organization has become part of the dominant economic and cultural pattern of our day.

Oddly enough, speculation concerning the course and character of American unionism has been remarkably wanting in the past two decades, during which the movement itself has experienced such impressive development and has been subjected to extensive investigation by both academicians and Congressional committees. Accumulation of facts has far outpaced reflection and interpretation. Indeed, theorizing about trade unionism in this country seems to have been practically stayed with the publication of Selig Perlman's *Theory of the Labor Movement* in 1928. Yet some analysis of the future course of American unions is necessary for intelligent long-run planning with respect to collective bargaining, labor legislation, and national economic policy.

Scope of Inquiry

This little volume examines the paths that organized labor in this country has been travelling and analyzes possible future trends. Primarily it is an investigation of the meaning and implications of union maturity in the American setting.

What factors influence the ageing of our unions? What moderates their militancy and hardens their arteries? What constitutes the settling-down process in labor organizations and how far will it progress? What are the socio-economics of advanced unionism? These are the sort of questions with which we shall be concerned.

Of necessity, our inquiry is focussed on the common strands that give direction to individual developments. Its approach is evolutionary and its aim is to arrive at generalizations that apply broadly over time. The intent is to weave a structure of conclusions out of the threads of experience within the labor movement and from the results of empirical research in industrial relations. The ultimate goal is a long-run theory of union evolution.

Attempting to develop a new interpretation of American unionism in long-range terms is, of course, a risky venture. Involved is the separation of fundamental from incidental or sporadic influences. Such a selective process obviously introduces the possibility of personal bias. The same is true of the emphasis placed on particular factors in union evolution. And the risk of oversimplification is likely to accompany forecasts of developments—even broad movements—within organized labor. Important external events which cannot be foreknown, such as war, may upset extrapolation of historic trends into the future. Such perils, however, are the occupational hazards of the long-run analyst in a field rich in interrelationships and influential factors.

Undoubtedly the difficulties and dangers attending such an effort largely explain why students of the labor movement have not constructed a systematic theory of union evolution. Professor R. F. Hoxie in his published lectures on *Trade Unionism in the United States* (1920) touched more than once on the question of internal change in unions. He explained that American unionism "is a developing process, and it is just this process of change and transition that the student must chiefly consider if he is to understand and interpret the phenomenon."[1] And again, after explaining that unionism follows a process of successive adaptations to a changing environment, Hoxie sets forth the operation of pairs of opposite tendencies as follows: "Union history shows a constant struggle between the forces of centralization and decentralization, autocracy and democracy, social idealism and enlightened self-interest, narrow trade autonomy and industrialism, economic and political method."[2] Regrettably, Hoxie did not reconcile or elaborate his diverse views on union development so that his occasional evolutionary generalizations were but interesting flashes of insight.

Somewhat more systematic interpretations of trade unionism have been advanced by Professors Selig Perlman and Frank Tannenbaum. However, neither of them focusses on continuing evolution and future trends. Perlman's theory of unionism is static rather than developmental. It rests on a normative psychology of "job-consciousness" in manual workers, which seemingly is universal in its application and unchanging over time.[3] In *A Philosophy of Labor* (1951), Tannenbaum deals with socio-psychological factors that help to explain the growth of unionism, which he considers to be the outcome of the workers' quest for security in a free market economy. But his interest is primarily historical. Tannenbaum does not attempt a systematic analysis of the institutional development of American unionism carried up to the present and projected into the future.

The studies previously mentioned have come from the pens of academicians. In December 1956, George W. Brooks, who for a dozen years has been Research Director of the Brotherhood of Pulp, Sulphite and Paper Mill Workers, presented a paper with a focus that approximates ours.[4] Entitled "Reflections on the Changing Character of American Labor Unions" and billed as "impressionistic," Brooks' remarks stressed three developments: (1) the shift of unions from militant opponents of management to elements in management's control system; (2) increased centralization of union affairs, under entrenched control by national headquarters; and (3) changes in the bargaining process, in the character of the leadership of national unions, and in the scale of values by which both leadership and membership measure union activities. Brooks, of course, made no pretense at developing a systematic theory. The rather extreme form in which some of his "broad generalizations" were couched seemed to indicate an intent to challenge, if not shock, fellow unionists in the audience at the 1956 meeting of the Industrial Relations Research Association. As the ensuing discussion proved, that purpose was accomplished.

The famous treatise on *Capitalism, Socialism and Democracy* (1942) by the late Professor Joseph A. Schumpeter has also been searched for possible guidance. Schumpeter attempted an evolutionary analysis of Western capitalism. He explained the factors and forces that, in his judgment, were leading to the decay of capitalism and its ultimate displacement by another economic system.

Unfortunately, Schumpeter's volume offers little in the way of a pattern for our analysis. Not only is it somewhat unsystematic and unstructured but its perspective is much broader. Schumpeter's vision and prognosis include capitalism throughout the Western World, and his reasoning is at a fairly high level of abstraction. The scope of our project is much more confined—to one country and to the institutional aspects of one sector of the economy.

Of course, organized labor cannot be completely abstracted from its economic and social environment. Indeed, some writers would claim that trade unionism and capitalism in this country are so joined together that they should not be analyzed apart from one another. The evolution of American capitalism, it would be contended, will determine the evolution of trade unionism in the United States. Hence, a correct long-run analysis of capitalism is a prerequisite to any long-run theory of trade unionism.

That is a fairly cogent contention. Labor unions are directly affected by industrial developments and management attitudes. It is for that reason that much of Chapter IV deals with management influences and that Chapter X discusses the joint aspects of the evolution of business corporations and unions.

However, all discrete investigations have to cope with the interrelatedness of things, and trade unions in America have now reached a stage of sufficient security and structural strength to warrant some independence of analysis. Moreover, they have ties not only to companies but also socially and politically, all of which means that any study of long-run institutional change in the labor movement should be well rounded as well as well grounded.

Plan of Book

At this point some indication of the book's coverage may help to orient the reader. The following sketch of chapters indicates their general content and their relationship to the principal objective of our pursuit, that is, to explain the factors in the evolution of American unionism.

The next chapter contains a brief discussion of the functions and character of unions, including some remarks on their political aspects. It provides a background for succeeding chapters.

The internal changes in American unions during recent decades are considered in broad terms in Chapter III.

Chapter IV covers the external factors that serve to integrate unions into the community and to broaden the interests of their leadership. It explains how management developments and the environmental setting have operated to promote moderation and reduce worker dissatisfaction.

The dynamic factors that tend to invigorate unions are examined in Chapter V. In analyzing the tendency for American unions to coast along, particular stress is placed on the reduction in union rivalry and in union opportunities for innovation.

Chapter vi looks into the corrupting influences within the labor movement, including the reduction of democratic checks, the tendency toward collaborative bargaining, and the tie-up between power and its abuse for personal profit.

The experience of trade unionism in England and Sweden —two countries with a fairly long experience with mature labor relations—is examined in Chapter vii for the light that developments in those countries can shed on long-run union theory.

In Chapter viii, the evolutionary experience of five important unions in this country is briefly summarized to bring out both the diversity and the common elements in their development.

The basic features of the theory of union evolution fashioned in the preceding chapters are summarized and refined in Chapter ix. This chapter is, in a sense, the keystone of the book.

Consideration of evolutionary trends is continued in Chapter x, where developments in management and in union-management relations are analyzed and used as a basis for some predictions.

The final two chapters develop the implications of the theory for economic analysis and for public policy, especially labor-relations legislation.

Most chapters contain summary paragraphs—usually at the end—and the chapters build upon one another. The reader must decide the extent to which such stacking has contributed to the accumulation of understanding or to the pyramiding of error.

This book is a think-piece in the sense that the conclusions in each chapter do not rest on one extensive research project. Rather, the book as a whole is based on over twenty years of study and analysis of industrial relations, especially collective bargaining.[5] Much of that time was spent in field investigations, in discussions and interviews with union and management officials, and in hearing and arbitrating labor disputes. Out of such experience one develops judgments that, although experience-based, cannot be specifically documented. Chapter vii rests primarily upon seventy interviews in England and thirty-five interviews in Sweden during four months spent in those countries in the Spring of 1956 with the specific purpose of this book in mind.[6] Nevertheless, judgments expressed in that chapter are as challengeable as those stated elsewhere in the book.

Studies and writings of others are offered in partial support of some of the book's conclusions. However, the writers referred to in the footnotes (placed at the end of the text) are in no way responsible for the conclusions developed in this volume.

Assumptions about the Future

This book is mainly concerned with an analysis of developments already experienced. Nevertheless predictions are expressed or implied at some points. It may, therefore, be appropriate to explain the principal assumptions upon which such predictions or projections rest.

One assumption is that general economic conditions over the next decade will be about the same as they have been during the past decade. That would mean relatively full employment, no severe depression, and an upward bias in the price level—a tendency for "creeping inflation." The underlying influences that have helped to produce these conditions —including high defense expenditures, rapid technological advance, marked population growth, and government price-support programs—seem likely to continue. Indeed, population pressures promise to be of greater influence over the next decade. While between 1955 and 1965 our total population will increase by 31 million, the working population is calculated to expand by but 10 million. Because of the low birth rates in the 1930's, the adult population from 25 to 44—the prime work ages—will not increase at all during that decade. Those figures, plus the possibility of a shortened work week, could mean a greater relative scarcity of labor up to 1965 than was experienced over the first post-war decade.

The second assumption is that during the next decade, organized labor will grow no faster than the total employed population expands. That has been true during the dozen years since 1945; organized labor has not expanded relatively. Good grounds exist for believing that, during the next decade, unions will not represent an increasing percentage of all wage and salary workers, given the economic conditions postulated above and the changing composition of the labor force.

Organized labor in this country consists largely of blue-collar workers, who are coming to represent a smaller percentage of total employment. The greatest expansion has been occurring in white-collar types of employment—professional, managerial, technical, administrative, and clerical. This trend toward more salaried relative to hourly-paid personnel in American industry seems likely to continue. One of the factors contributing to it is heavy investment in equipment, including automation. Another factor is the continuing expansion in consumer demand for services relative to manufactured goods. For a variety of reasons, including status, aims, and nearness to management, white-collar workers have generally resisted joining labor unions, particularly those dominated by production workers. No grounds exist for expecting a significant change in the response of white-collar workers to the appeals of trade unionism over the ensuing decade.

The third assumption is that the American labor movement will continue to have a single central federation and will not be split into rival union centers as it was from 1935 to 1955. During the early part of that period, rivalry between the CIO and the AFL provided a special stimulus to new organization, and helped to invigorate the whole movement. Affiliation of most of organized labor to one national center seems to be in the American tradition and has been traditional in such countries as Britain, Sweden, Norway, Denmark, Holland, Australia, and New Zealand. At this writing, however, a threat exists that the unions expelled from the AFL-CIO on charges of corruption may attempt to form a rival federation under the Teamsters' leadership. In view of the strength and position of the Teamsters' union, such a development could have wide repercussions and would stimulate competition in new organization. Even so, one would not expect any great extension of unionism into areas now unorganized.

If the future conforms to the above assumptions, trends in American unionism experienced over the past decade (1948-1957) may be expected to continue without too much change over the next decade. Even some deviations from the assumptions might produce little alteration in the general pattern of union development. However, a significant upset could bring about marked changes within the labor movement. These three broad assumptions should, therefore, be considered more as analytical guidelines than as firm forecasts of actual developments. Their purpose is to aid in the task of analysis, to which we now turn.

II. THE ESSENCE OF UNIONISM

THIS CHAPTER attempts to set forth the rationale for American trade unionism. What kind of an organism is a union? What basic functions do labor organizations perform? What role do they play in our society? Answers to those questions should provide a framework and some benchmarks for our analysis of evolutionary change in unions in the United States.

Labor organization has a long history in America. The first unions were formed in the 1790's and hence preceded the first business corporations. They were home-grown products that arose out of workers' pursuit of their self-interests in the workshop. By organization, the craftsmen sought to protect and promote the value of their skilled training. Over a century and a half ago it was evident that wage-earners had interests at times opposed to those of employers, creditors, or consumers.

Factory employment requires the worker to place himself under the direction and authority of the firm's management. In each industrial plant, there are managers and the managed, whose work experience and viewpoints differ. The one gives the orders which the others follow under a definitely understood system of industrial discipline. The managed have a relatively low social status, outside as well as inside the plant, but in the home, in the community, or in political affairs they are not subject to the stratification and authority inherent in a large business organization.

It is not surprising that factory stratification, discipline, and chain of command create worker irritations, dissatisfactions, and protest. In a democratic society with emphasis on material well-being and advancement, wage-earners at the base of the industrial hierarchy tend to accumulate a variety of real and fancied grievances against management. They may think that they have been unjustly treated by the foremen, that their good qualities are not properly appreciated and rewarded, or that the management is trying to take advantage of their weak economic position. Union people explain that even good managements can be counted on to cause some employee ill-will by decisions regarding lay-off, transfer, promotion, and other aspects of job assignment. Resentment against management is found not only in private industry but in plants that are publicly owned and operated. Indeed, it exists to a degree wherever some men are managed by others.

Unions stress the personal and political, as well as the economic, aspects of industry. They seek to reduce the human costs of production by such means as helping to protect workers from arbitrary or discriminatory decisions of management, improving the employees' peace of mind through greater job security, and raising the level of dignity and respect with which wage-earners are treated in the plant. Through a union, the members achieve a status and a feeling that they count for something, that they are not just little cogs in a large and impersonal wheel of industry. Of course, management also may seek to promote worker contentment and human relations in the plant—at least within the limits of management's views of its own rights, responsibilities, and goals.

Furthermore, one's place in the industrial hierarchy tends to influence his social philosophy, so that differences in work position and experience are reflected in economic and political orientation.[1] Unskilled and semi-skilled workers, for example, seem prone to stress group values such as security and government action, whereas persons in corporate management generally favor individualism and market solutions to economic problems.[2] It is understandable, therefore, that on issues such as wages and tax policy, workers tend to hold views different from those of management, and that union leaders and management spokesmen frequently are on the opposite sides of economic and political questions.

Bargaining and Political Aspects

Unions serve as a channel and administrative agency for worker protest.[3] Through collective bargaining, grievance procedures, and a practical monopoly of the strike, they have come to exercise a proprietary interest over labor protest. Of course, other contenders, including political leaders, the government, religious leaders, and business organizations, strive to share in the function of expressing and satisfying workers' discontent and aspirations. And as workers' needs and desires assume a greater political and social content, unions have tended to broaden their service activities accordingly.

Nowadays a labor union establishes its position and bargaining rights not so much by its economic powers as by its political appeal. It achieves certification by the National Labor Relations Board as sole bargaining agent at a plant by winning an election rather than by winning a strike. And once certified, the union and its leaders continue as a politically structured institution in competition with an authoritarian-directed and largely economic-oriented corporation.[4] The competition between unions and their leaders on the one side and management and corporations on the other is not only in terms of employee allegiance or loyalties but also in terms of differences in concepts, values, and goals.

A labor union is a political organization representing the members' job interests and their viewpoints on political and social issues. Basically it is a conflict organization, with separate traditions, loyalties, and leadership, which is intent upon improving the union's prestige and power. Leaders of such democratic-structured organizations as unions are, of course, under pressure to give expression to and devise programs for the latent discontent among the membership. Moreover, as elected officials, trade-union leaders must consider the possibility of rivals unseating them in some future ballot. When the leadership is nonresponsive and the union outlets become ineffective, workers' discontent and protest may take such suppressed forms as work slowdowns or may break out in wildcat strikes in opposition to the national leadership of the union. Because industrial change stirs workers and because satisfaction is a relative state—based on what one wants, expects, and sees others enjoying—improvements in the general level of living do not necessarily eliminate a significant part of the protest element among worker groups.[5]

In recent decades, worker protest against management has tended to extend beyond the workshop. It has taken such forms as political disagreement, struggle against dominance of the community by management elements, and opposition to the creed and value systems of business, which have exerted such a controlling influence in our society. Union representation of labor's complaints and aspirations not only in the plant but also in political and social affairs results in unions taking positions on all sorts of political issues and entering into local activities such as the community chest and other welfare programs.[6]

Understandably, as unions seek more and more to represent not only the job problems but also the political and social aspirations of workers, they come into competition with other institutions such as political parties, churches, chambers of commerce, civic organizations, medical associations, and even insurance companies. But expansion in the scope of their functions also causes unions to seek approval of the general public for such broadened activities and to try to win allies among some of their potential competitors for representation of workers' protest, such as liberal organizations, political groups, and religious leaders.

Any active organization founded with a mission is, of course, continuously in the process of redefining and reinterpreting its purposes and functions as it settles down and its environment changes. In the process of adaptation, new balances are drawn among the various objectives and interest areas of a union, and, at any one time, various echelons of the union may, generally speaking, have somewhat different conceptions of the proper aims and role of the union. By and large, a union's rank-and-file members tend to stress job-centered activities, particularly collective bargaining, which assumes a core of conflicting interests between the parties, and grievance handling, which focusses on individual protest and protection. The "activists" at the local level, and especially the full-time officials at the national level of the union, are more prone to press for a wider range of activities and to stress the long-run interest of the trade-union movement as a whole. Such a difference in horizon is understandable. Collective bargaining normally results directly in better pay, working conditions, or both. The rewards of union political activity, on the other hand, are likely to be both uncertain and obscure. Partly this is because political representation is much broader than trade-union representation and the connections between voting, legislation, and worker self-interest are often difficult to unravel and assess. Nevertheless, despite significant setbacks, union political activity seems, generally speaking, to have expanded in scope during the last decade or so.[7]

Sometimes the question has been asked whether unions are political or economic institutions, as though the two were somehow mutually exclusive. Actually the internal processes of unions are mainly political, but the issues handled are often economic. In that regard, unions are like political parties, whose platforms consist chiefly of bread-and-butter issues but which deal with economic questions mainly in political terms.

Indeed, in many respects, a union resembles a political party. It has an ideology and traditions, a national organization and local branches, and conflicts of interest among the membership. Much of its local activity consists of handling personal grievances and protests. Usually only 5 to 10 per cent of the membership are "actives," who participate in the union's administration, policy decisions, and meetings. Elections play a significant role—elections for certification as bargaining agent, election of officers, strike ballots, and votes on policies, programs, or constitutional changes. The negotiation of a new agreement or an organization drive is similar in various respects to a political campaign. The opposition of a union consists of management rather than an opposing political party but both a union and a political organization have a problem of accommodation after each contest. Obviously, there are also differences between the two types of organizations. However, it is important to bear in mind that a union is a politically-operated institution, with a political leadership and often a personal political machine built on the patronage available in the national union. As is explained more fully in a later chapter, union leaders in countries like England and Sweden lack the personal powers of appointment and control that the presidents of most of our national unions enjoy. One consequence is the greater possibility of use of union office for personal gain in this country.

Role in Democratic Society

By guiding workers' discontent into orderly channels for its relief and by competing with other organizations for the representation of workers' varied interests, unions perform a beneficial role in a democratic society. Unions, by aiding in the reconciliation of conflicting interests, contribute to constructive social change.[8] Collective bargaining, ideally, is a mutual exploration of differences, based on the facts, and a willingness to be convinced and to compromise temporarily. To be successful it must be a process of mutual education; both sides must explain the reasons for their positions and why the claims or position of the other party cannot be adopted in full. The parties must be open-minded and interested in investigating and solving problems if the socially beneficial values of collective bargaining are to be achieved.

Within a union, the active rank-and-file members need to participate in the formulation of demands and in the process of negotiating and accepting the terms of settlement. Collective bargaining loses its educational value if this group does not genuinely participate in the processes that lead to the bargaining outcome, if by some "deal" in advance of bargaining or by mere role playing on the part of spokesmen for both sides, the conflicts of interest are not examined and reconciled through democratic procedures on the union side. Our economic system, as well as our political system, rests on the cooperation and consent of the governed—industrially, the managed employees. If the local leaders and rank-and-file do not understand and accept the terms that are negotiated for employment in the plant, collective bargaining has failed, just as the two-party system of politics fails when campaigns are so one-sided that criticism and debate on the issues are absent.

True, certification as sole bargaining agent and the necessity for management to gain the consent of its employees may give the union some temporary advantages in bargaining. But unions are only as strong as their leadership and membership. It has been claimed that unions seek to achieve monopoly. The question is: a monopoly of what? Bargaining rights? They get that by NLRB certification. Of the labor supply? Nowadays that is practically impossible in most industries, and under the Taft-Hartley Act the employer's right to hire cannot be restricted by the union shop.

Labor agreements do contain job control features but they are the result of mutual negotiation and can be changed by the same process. Complete control over wages by a union is certainly much more unusual than is such control by management under nonunion conditions.[9]

Although one may find cases, especially in local-market lines, in which union control of jobs or over wages approaches monopoly power, it is important to consider the checks on any such absolute power and to bear in mind the various kinds of competition that may confront any institution seeking to represent labor protest. In a subsequent chapter, such competition—intra-union, interunion, and interinstitutional—is examined as a factor in the evolution of the life of unions. That sort of potential competition, although perhaps declining somewhat in recent years, is more significant than most economists recognize. Indeed, institutional competition for labor representation largely falls outside the economists' concept of competition, which is drawn in market terms.

In considering the essential features of American trade unionism one must, of course, bear in mind the wide variation of individual unions from what might be called the center or core of our labor movement. Some unions, such as the building trades, place great emphasis on job control and thus have a comparatively narrow scope of interests and activities. Others, like the United Auto Workers, have a wide-ranging leadership that stresses the importance of political action. Such differences among individual unions arise not only from contrasts in the industrial environment of particular unions—local versus national markets, the size of firms, production techniques, and so forth—but also may be influenced by historical roots that extend back to the formative years of the union.

This chapter has attempted to set forth the essential characteristics of American unionism, the features that are at or near the core of our labor movement. To understand labor organizations, it is necessary to appreciate the conflict of interests and the differences in social philosophy between management and managed. The union serves as a channel and instrument for worker protest. Internally it is essentially a political organization, whose operations often extend beyond the job into political and community activities. Naturally unions compete with other institutions and elements in the community for a share in the representation of workers' interests. Unions themselves are not monolithic but contain groups with differing viewpoints and, as the environment changes, union goals are frequently redefined. Successful collective bargaining is an educational process that aids in such redefinition of union objectives and purposes. In so far as unions perform educational functions and help to reconcile conflicts of interest, they serve a beneficial role in a democratic society.

III. THE CHANGING CHARACTER
OF AMERICAN UNIONISM

SINCE THE MID-1930's, unions in this country have experienced certain internal changes. Many, especially the newly formed industrial unions, have been shedding youthful characteristics in the process of settling down or "maturing."

Some support exists for the theory that institutions tend to pass through stages of development, that organizations like unions, which aim at altering the balance of rights and privileges, experience a natural evolution of organizational life, particularly if they are successful. In their early stages such organizations will be militant and turbulent, with internal factionalism and vigorous external opposition. At first they must fight for existence as well as for goals that generally are considered radical. Under the circumstances membership participation is likely to be high and leadership positions in the organization are apt to be won by the agitator and the table-pounder.

Later on, as the organization gains acceptance and security and succeeds in establishing new rights and other aims, a transformation tends to occur not only in the organization's goals but also in the nature of its leadership, in its internal operations, and in the distribution of power and functions among different structural levels. Instead of being simply an opposition or anti-body, the new organization becomes more and more integrated into the life of the community. Instead of pursuing a crusade against the "enemy," it cooperates increasingly with other groups in industry, government, and society. As some of the organization's initial goals are

[21]

achieved, its objectives tend to broaden and become more complex, so that they are increasingly difficult to define and delimit. As the organization grows in size and its activities and responsibilities enlarge, it faces new problems of administration, discipline, and public relations. The need for specialists becomes more pressing, a hierarchy and bureaucracy tend to develop, and the relationship of top officials to the rank-and-file grows more impersonal. Some functions and decisions shift from the local to higher levels in the organization. And, as the top positions come to require more administrative and manipulative talents, the oratorical agitators are superseded by skillful managers.

Of course, every organization, even every one for improving the lot of labor, does not have the same life history. There is no one inevitable pattern of metamorphosis, no single evolutionary route. Each organization is influenced by its own circumstances and experience—the way it was formed, the traditions it has developed, the industrial challenges it has faced, the sort of opposition it has encountered, and the character of the growth it has achieved. Certain general factors may, of course, affect all organizations, albeit unevenly. For instance, within a large organization with officers selected by ballot, a political machine tends to develop, but that does not mean political parties and unions inevitably end up controlled by a ruling clique as postulated by Robert Michels' "iron law of oligarchy."[1] Not only must one recognize that various underlying forces may not all push in the same direction but also that considerable deviation from any trend is to be expected in the case of institutions with diverse historical experiences such as trade unions.

Internally, three significant changes have occurred in American unions in recent decades. In many unions, greater centralization has developed with the transfer of functions and decisions from the locals to national headquarters. Second, the status and outlook of top union leaders has been changing with increased size, stability, and responsibilities. Third, union militancy and demagoguery have tended to give way to carefully prepared presentations and disciplined representation. These three changes could be considered parts of a single development—achievement of the union's early goals for organization and for collective bargaining. On the other hand, the three changes are the broad consequences of various factors and trends, which need to be examined in order to understand the undercurrents that have helped to shape the course of union developments. This chapter is largely devoted to such an analysis.

Centralization of Functions and Control

A number of factors have been instrumental in shifting some functions, decisions, and power from the local level to the national headquarters of unions.

In the first place, expansion of the size of the national union, by means of growth in the number of locals and perhaps by merger also, serves to reduce the importance and influence of a particular local within the union. Furthermore the larger the national union, the more patronage there is by which to build up a political machine with control from the top, and the more union communications (including publications) are likely to be centrally controlled. Also, large unions tend to have comparatively large staffs of specialists and experts, upon whom locals come to rely for guidance. Indeed, the assumption generally is made that, with unions, large size means more effectiveness, efficiency, and power. That assumption stems partly from the notion that a larger union can hire a bigger and better staff, partly from the gain to be achieved from central pooling of resources such as strike funds, but partly also from the naïve notion that size and power are directly correlated.

Expansion in the area of collective bargaining and enlargement of the spread of bargaining patterns have also contributed to central determination of union policies. The national seeks a common program for the whole industry or area of competitive production. Bargaining strategy necessitates some central control of demands, along with headquarters' approval of settlements negotiated by locals and of strikes by locals. In short, union-wide programs increase the influence and authority of the national headquarters.

A change in the character and subject matter of negotiations has likewise added to the dependence of the locals on the top echelon of the union. Collective bargaining has tended to be increasingly factual, statistical, and full of economic reasoning, so that the amateur negotiator feels himself at a disadvantage. But it is particularly the technical nature of the new subjects in negotiations that has increased the role of the national headquarters and the staff. Subjects like job evaluation, time-and-motion study, pensions, medical and hospital care, and supplementary unemployment benefits, are generally beyond the training and know-how of persons at the local level. For guidance in such matters, the union may need to rely upon the advice of staff experts.

National labor legislation, intervention in industrial relations by Federal agencies, and reliance upon arbitration also increase the dependence on experts, especially lawyers and economists, attached to the national headquarters and appointed by the top officials. The Taft-Hartley Act is a complex piece of legislation, on many aspects of which legal advice may be necessary before a union makes a decision. Appearances before Federal agencies (National War Labor Board, Wage Stabilization Board, Atomic Energy Labor-Management Relations Panel, etc.) are generally a function performed by the national union. In addition, national union officers or staff members are likely to play a dominant role in significant arbitration cases, including grievance arbitrations.

The role of local union leaders has been reduced with the

shift of the center of union activities from organization to disciplined administration of the agreement and with the newer methods of organization and dues collection: namely, certification by the National Labor Relations Board, the union shop, and the check-off of dues.

Prior to World War II, much of the time of the local union leaders in the mass-production industries was taken up with maintaining and increasing the membership and collecting dues. Now employers do most of that for the union, by enforcing the union shop and deducting the dues from workers' wages for the union. On the other hand, the union helps the management to enforce the shop rules and plant discipline by insistence on no violation of the agreement. Such a partial swapping of functions has resulted in a reduction of the power and authority of shop stewards and other local leaders. No longer can they call men out on strike without the national union demanding that the strike be revoked as a violation of the agreement, the union's constitution, or both. In the case of grievances, which now are likely to be the bulk of the local's business, not only must they be handled in an orderly and businesslike fashion, but the national union may have a hand in them at a fairly early stage because it assumes responsibility in the final steps of the grievance procedure. Thus, compared with the 1930's, local unions now generally serve less as independent centers of leadership and decision-making and more as the administrative agencies of the national union.[2]

The No-raiding Pact, the AFL-CIO merger, national union mergers, and other restrictions on change of local-union affiliation have also helped to reduce the independence of action and the bargaining power of the locals within their national unions. With rival national unions and national federations, the locals of any union could threaten to leave it and affiliate with a rival union, if the national disregarded the local's wishes or sought to restrict and dominate it. No longer is that a possibility for most locals. Higher authority denies them freedom of affiliation.

Although in recent decades the centripetal forces have tended to expand at the expense of centrifugal factors in most unions, some have succeeded in maintaining a balance between them. For the most part, however, only unions in local-market lines with numerous small firms, like the building trades, have been able to do so. Other unions, such as the Teamsters, have experienced a strengthening of the regional or district units at the expense of the locals, but with comparatively slight gains in headquarters power and control. Along with the character of the industry, the traditions of the union and its historical development may help to determine the location of union control and decision-making power and the extent to which they have been moving toward and into the union's national headquarters.

Alteration in Top Leadership

As unions expand and become accepted by the community, subtle changes tend to occur in their top leadership. The founding fathers and the early recruits with a missionary zeal die or retire with the passage of time. They are replaced by a second or third generation of leaders, who personally have not experienced the bitter struggles for existence in the union's early days and who are less likely to have had the influences of an immigrant background or socialist convictions in their youth. As already indicated, such successors tend to be, not the crusading agitator, but the skillful political operator and level-headed administrator able to manage a large organization and to perform the necessary desk duties.[3] The president of a union has a variety of administrative responsibilities. Among other things, he is the employer of a staff, the head of a political machine, and the highest union authority in the enforcement of collective agreements.

As unions settle down, the path to top leadership tends to

be a steady climb through the various levels of the hierarchy. Stratification in organizations generally increases with their size and age. In mature organizations, the selection and training of leaders at the lower levels are likely to be controlled from the top. High union officials are organization men, who are prone to stress unity and to frown on insurgency. The prospects for advancement may also discourage insurgency. Mobility within the labor movement is largely vertical in one national union; seldom do union leaders transfer from one union to another, which might imply some lack of loyalty to the union's administration. Yet as unions mature, their growth curve tends to flatten out, which means that advancement is largely confined to replacements in the hierarchy, and such replacement openings are reduced by the absence of a specific retirement age similar to that in British and Swedish unions. This organizational development, of course, affects attitudes at various levels in the institution.

The promotional outlook is, however, but one aspect of the psychological change which is likely to occur. The gap between the members' wages and the salaries of the presidents of the larger unions has increased relatively during the 1940's and 1950's. The heads of the dozen largest unions have salaries ranging from $18,000 to $60,000 a year, plus ample expense accounts and frequently other perquisites. That union presidents sometimes urge conventions not to increase their salaries does not alter the fact that it is possible for them to live on a scale equivalent to that of business executives and that, in the newly-built union headquarters, the presidential officers are as impressive as those of high corporate officials.[4]

Nowadays the presidency of a union carries a wide range of duties and responsibilities. The concept of the office has broadened as union presidents have increasingly held positions on community, industrial, educational, and governmental boards. The president of a sizeable union may be expected to make pronouncements on national economic policy, foreign policy, domestic politics, and all sorts of legislative proposals as well as the problems of his industry. Many of his activities might be considered extraunion, and in connection with them he associates with leaders in all walks of life.

As full-time union officials progress up the union hierarchy their interests and perspectives tend to broaden. Over the years, the scope of union activities has been enlarging, which has meant an increase in the "sobering responsibilities" of the presidency. For instance, he may shoulder the ultimate responsibility for the investment of the growing union and joint funds. Their financial interests have led unions to participate in the banking, insurance, and real estate businesses, to say nothing of investments in stocks and bonds.

Many union leaders in the past have been unconventionally motivated—men with a mission to alter the economic and social order, with little thought of personal gain. There are indications that the concept of the successful union president may have been changing somewhat in the 1940's and 1950's, even in the minds of many holding that office. As their interests and associations have broadened, they may place more stress on their reputations with the general public.

Of course, the union official is a politician with a definite constituency. To continue in office he has to be reelected by the membership or their chosen delegates in convention assembled. He must, therefore, be sensitive to membership views and discontents. The leadership of a union is under pressure to achieve material gains for the membership, to make a "breakthrough" that will increase the prestige of the union compared with other unions.

The role of the union president is, however, somewhat ambivalent. At the same time that he desires to negotiate noteworthy gains, he also strongly wishes to achieve a settlement without a strike that could threaten the security of the present leadership or of the union itself. Part of the union leader's job, therefore, is mediating and working out satisfactory compromises. Above all, he assumes responsibility for enforcing agreements, for upholding the sanctity of contracts even though that means disciplining malcontented elements within the union membership. By insisting on the use of orderly settlement procedures and preventing wildcat strikes, he joins with management in maintaining discipline within the plant.

Changes in the concept of union leadership at headquarters do, of course, work their way down the line. Not only are union presidents spending more time in community and governmental activities but so are full-time officials in the lower ranks. And conceptions at the lower levels are influenced by the fact that those seeking to advance into the charmed circle at the top tend to conform to the aims and viewpoints of their superiors.[5]

In discussing the tendency for union leadership to evolve in certain directions it should be clear that there is no compulsion for all union headquarters to conform to a single pattern. However, factors have been at work which are influencing the evolution of union leadership. Unless new factors—such as a severe business depression, upsetting internal crises in particular unions, or perhaps a war—arise to alter the direction of the drift, the differences between union executives and business executives in living standards, in daily activities, and in business interests, are likely to continue to diminish.

Decline in Militancy

Generally speaking, unions have lost some of the militancy and rambunctiousness that characterized them before World War II. During the 1940's and 1950's they became more disciplined and businesslike.

[29]

Opinions differ as to the circumstances and factors responsible for such "taming" of American unions. Doubtless the developments already discussed—centralization of control and changes in union leadership—have been contributing factors. But, equally if not more important have been certain developments outside the union that are examined in the next chapter, namely, greater employer acceptance and cooperation with labor organizations, the increase in workers' living standards under full employment, and the growth of moderation and middle-of-the-road attitudes in American society during the postwar years.[6]

Union militancy is, of course, one reaction to employer hostility and threats to the union's existence. Unions also tend to be aggressively active when their security is challenged by government, by left wing competitors, or by internal troubles and rebellion. Indeed, as the main channel for worker protest, they are agitated by any increase in employee discontent whether arising from unemployment, technological change, or arbitrary management decisions.

Labor leaders stress new organization, strikes, and grievances as sources of union vigor and vitality. The expansion of organization to new plants and areas brings into the union's fold recruits who have been combatting employer opposition and have the crusading spirit. Thus the infusion of new blood imbued with the old fervor helps to rejuvenate the union. Similarly the founding of new unions and the rapid growth of others, as in the mass production industries in the 1930's, stimulate older unions like those in building, railroads, and printing. By pushing ahead with new ideas and gains, the growing areas provide competition and a dynamic quality that spreads through the movement.

A strike, by providing an emotional outlet as well as an economic contest, may serve to rekindle some of the militant spirit of the union's pioneering period. The membership is emotionally stirred up by a struggle and out of it new leaders may arise to challenge the national union's leadership. In fact, some strikes are not only against the company but also in opposition to the headquarters' policies and control of the union.

Grievances, which are protests against management decisions under the agreement, also represent a contest and help to keep the local union active and agitated. They usually play a significant role in the political life of locals, where contests for office and turnover of officials are generally more frequent than at the national level. Ferment in a union is usually concentrated in the active group in locals, consisting of perhaps 3 to 10 per cent of the membership, which is occupied largely with the grievance complaints of members.

The adventurous and demanding quality of the American worker, which strikes European students of industrial relations,[7] supplies a force for change at the local level. A people, stemming from immigrants who protested against authority in Europe and developed self-reliance in frontier communities, may be quick to take forceful action in pursuit of their demands. Of course, the longer they are accustomed to settled, suburban living the more conditioned they may be against resort to violent protests.

The passage of time and generations does seem to have strengthened various factors that tend to "calm down" our unions and their leaders. The success of unions in establishing rights and in negotiating gains has served, in most industries, to reduce the "core of conflict" and to contract the uncharted areas where unions might present new challenges to management rights. Indeed, as managements accept unions, consult with them about solutions to problems, and seek constructive labor relations, many of the pressing difficulties become adjusted.

Of course, settlement of most of the big issues does not eliminate grievances, for foremen are human and the establishment of new piece rates is often a contentious matter.

However, collective bargaining institutionalizes conflict by gradually building up orderly processes, joint machinery, and other administrative restraints against unruly or precipitate action. The United Mine Workers provides an example of such restraints. In May 1956, John Lewis and the UMW executive board sent notice to all miners stating that unauthorized stoppages were in violation of union policy, that the machinery of the joint agreement must be used to settle disputes, and that fines would be levied on the treasuries of locals which engaged in unauthorized work stoppages. At the UMW convention in October 1956, Mr. Lewis announced that such fines had been levied, that the union would act to protect men observing the contract, and that repeated violations of the UMW policy would bring stiffer fines and perhaps also charges by the national union against the leaders and instigators of such strikes. The *Daily Labor Report* commented on this development: "This may be hard for some of the old timers to assimilate, but major coal bargaining is no longer a matter of open strife between Lewis and the operators. The bargainers sit within a block of each other the year around; negotiations are kept secret until word of the end result 'leaks' out."[8]

Other developments have also served to discourage local insurgency. Left wing unionism has been unpopular since World War II. Not only has the Socialist Party shrunk almost to a shadow, but many of the Communist-dominated unions have dwindled or disintegrated. The consequence is that American unions have little left wing competition, no serious challenges from radical rivals seeking to woo their membership or the unorganized. Furthermore, the AFL-CIO merger has banned competition for locals among the affiliated national unions, with the result that a local cannot escape the domination of a political machine in control of a national union by threatening to seek attachment to another national union.

[32]

The reinvigorating effects of new organization and strikes for rights have been explained. Failure to extend organization into significant new territory during the years since World War II has meant that the new spirit resulting from enlarged organization has been largely lacking in the American labor movement during the postwar period. Furthermore, strikes generally have become much less emotional and rancorous than they were before World War II or even in the late 1940's. Not infrequently, picketing is unnecessary now, or the management supplies pickets with conveniences like hot coffee and coal for heat on cold days. In the 1956 steel strike, for example, United States Steel at several plants provided the pickets with mobile toilets and at one plant even ran a power line and water to the union's six trailers.[9] Under such circumstances, the strike becomes almost a friendly difference conducted in an orderly manner with good will on both sides. The decline in union militancy is easy to understand.

One must, of course, recognize that in matters such as new organization, strikes, and left wing challenges, the development is uneven and individual unions may have experience at variance with the general drift. Some unions still are somewhat insecure either because of the significance of non-union competition, employer opposition, or other conditions in their industries. And within a union, there may be wide variation in attitudes and stage of development, with rather bitter skirmishes at union outposts in the South or in rural areas. And always the possibility exists that developments such as economic depression, automation, legislation, or large-scale organization, may stir things up sufficiently within the labor movement so as to cause an alteration or even some reversal in the main drift—at least temporarily.

In concluding this chapter on internal aspects of union evolution it should be stressed that our concern has been

[33]

with underlying and long-run tendencies. In some national unions these gradual developments have progressed further than in others; within a single union, some sections may evidence more "maturity" than other sections. It is a matter of degree, with considerable variation and some counteracting forces.

The three currents or strands of development that were examined must be viewed in proper perspective. Centralization is only a tendency. Some issues, such as seniority and production standards, probably will always have to be handled at the local level. Some reduction in the cultural and motivational differences between union and management leaders does not mean that significant differences do not or will not continue to exist. To say that union militancy seems to be waning does not deny the fact that unions still present and prosecute grievances with vigor or imply that strikes are obsolete. Indeed, the number of grievances has actually increased in recent years in some automobile and rubber companies. What the settling-down process does mean, however, is that union behavior has been changing; for example, voting for recognition has largely replaced striking for it and the "challenges" (to use Toynbee's term) which face the union have been modified as left wing unionism and dual unionism have given way to a more unified labor movement.

Times change and so do labor organizations. It is important to observe the extent to which the strands of change conform to some pattern of development, to discover the elements of unity in apparent diversity. The next chapter considers the external factors that have been influencing the evolution of unions in this country in certain directions.

IV. MANAGEMENT AND OTHER EXTERNAL INFLUENCES

ENVIRONMENTAL CONDITIONS affect unions in various ways. This chapter deals with the influences that external factors— changes in management, in economic conditions, in governmental policies, and in the community and the cultural climate—exert on unions and their programs.

The opinion has often been expressed that environmental factors have contributed greatly to the maturing process within unions. Such developments as more enlightened management, high employment levels and rising living standards, and increasing integration of unions into the community, it is claimed, have progressively reduced worker dissatisfaction, lessened class consciousness, and broadened union interests. Continued union-management negotiations and agreements, it is said, have increasingly served to institutionalize disagreement, narrow the area of conflict, and stabilize industrial relations. Optimists assume that such environmental changes have wrought long-run alterations in union-management relations and in unions themselves.

Other students of unions remain unconvinced that environmental conditions have brought about a definite trend toward industrial tranquility and union moderation. The environment, they point out, can change in ways that may reverse the recent drift. In their view, the developments of the past decade are not evidence of a new era but are a phase in a cycle of dynamic disturbance and assimilating adjustment, which fluctuates around a horizontal trend pointing in no particular direction. Since 1946, they say, we have been in a period of consolidation and relative calm. However, the basic conflicts of interest between labor and management, the institutional competition between unions and business organizations, and the power struggles between groups still remain; sooner or later, these critics contend, dynamic changes in industry and society—whether automation, business depression, white-collar discontent, or what not—will produce new strains and another period of worker unrest and union militancy. Nor will such a resurgence be prevented by improvements in the general level of living, for worker dissatisfaction arises largely from assumed inequities and current aspirations and comparisons. Hence one should expect undulations and shifts of direction rather than advance along a more or less steady course.[1]

The correctness of these differing views is not easy to determine. Basically the issue is the extent to which recent developments in unions and in labor-management relations are the result of short-run and cyclical factors or are a consequence of long-term influences and trends. Historically, periods of relative tranquility have been followed by times of unrest, generated by a new constellation of forces. Nevertheless, changes have occurred in some aspects of industry, government, and society since 1900—changes whose direction seems irreversible and which have significance for the future of industrial relations. Definite determination of the long-range importance that particular changes have for unions may, however, be complicated by international developments, such as the cold war, whose future is beclouded by uncertainty.

Moreover, a process like collective bargaining produces consequences that vary with the circumstances. It is both a dynamic, disrupting force and a stabilizing, orderly influence. Union leadership may either stir up or play down worker protest. The environment will have a significant influence on the dominant features of union activity—whether stress is on the union as a militant opponent of management or a responsible representative with fairly wide interests.

The external influences on American unions will be discussed in this chapter under six headings: changes in management, developments in bargaining relationships, general economic conditions, the cultural climate, community interests and integration, and political challenge and action. Under each heading an attempt will be made to determine the extent to which the factors under analysis are short-range phenomena or long-term trends.

Changes in Management

Management's philosophy of industrial relations has been changing over time, particularly at the plant level. Since the beginning of this century, significant shifts have occurred in the concept of employment. Broadly speaking, and especially in larger firms, the "commodity concept" of labor freely and callously bought on a short-run basis under competitive conditions has given way to a more humane conception, influenced by psychological and welfare considerations, with stress on job satisfaction and worklife attachment to the firm.

The changing concept of employment is reflected in the succession of industrial relations programs or approaches that gained wide acceptance in the three decades prior to World War II. The first was scientific management or Taylorism,[2] which came into vogue in the decade from 1910 to 1920. Based on systematic job analysis, time study of job performance, and standardization of job operations, its mechanistic bias seemed suited to the current attitude toward and treatment of plant employees, many of whom were recent immigrants who spoke only broken English. The second program was the development in the 1920's of personnel management and welfare capitalism. Containing overtones of management paternalism, it stressed a battery of techniques including employee representation, profit-sharing, stock ownership, suggestion systems, company magazines, and benefit programs such as group life insurance, pensions, and sickness pay. In this approach, management concern for the individual welfare and loyalty of plant employees becomes evident. That concern is given additional emphasis in the "human relations" approach that began to capture management thinking in the 1930's. Drawing on studies by Harvard Business School professors at the Hawthorne plant of Western Electric,[3] the human relations movement is based in good part on applied psychology. Initially the therapeutic value of individual interviewing, employee counselling, and small group communication was emphasized. Later this "new image of the worker" as a personality whose inner feelings need expression and respectful treatment, led to a broader range of company activities designed to improve employee satisfaction on and off the job.

In practice these three strands of industrial relations philosophy are not, of course, so sharply distinguished either in time period or in management thinking as the above exposition might seem to imply. For instance, scientific management techniques continue to be widely applied in industry. However, their application may be modified, qualified, and supplemented if the "human relations" philosophy holds sway in top management of the firm.

Since the 1930's no new approach in industrial relations has gained widespread acceptance in basic industry. The three pre-World War II philosophies developed apart from trade unionism and initially they envisioned no particular or continuing role for unions to play. During the 1940's and 1950's, the labor problems of large-scale industry primarily involved accommodation to the existence and programs of unions. To some extent, the initiative in industrial relations had shifted from management to unions. In addition, developments in the social sciences failed to provide the basis for a new philosophical approach. As a consequence, a variety of management philosophies of labor relations have prevailed, ranging from union-management cooperation and working harmony to union containment and union circumvention by cultivating direct management-employee communication.

The question has been raised whether any basic change has occurred in management's philosophy toward unions or whether only its tactics have altered as management's understanding has improved.[4]

Undoubtedly American managers have become more expert and professional in the field of industrial relations during recent decades. Industrial relations departments of firms have grown relatively in size and status. Supervisory selection, training, and practices have improved. In the plant, persuasion and participation have been displacing authoritarian methods of management, as companies have experimented with human relations techniques and have utilized the results of research in morale. Most managements have come to recognize the benefits of a satisfactory handling of grievances. In various ways, union policies and activities have stimulated improvements in management that have resulted in more just and equitable treatment of production workers. In addition, managements have gained a much better understanding of unions, and, consequently, are in a position to anticipate union actions and reactions.

Intelligence, however, may alter means but not ends. Have the attitudes of American management toward employees and toward unions experienced a basic change that will not be wiped out by future development?

Certainly management's treatment of employees as individuals has, generally speaking, changed in an irreversible manner.[5] Its shock from the revolt of labor in the 1930's, when workers flocked into unions, may have been largely temporary, but the ensuing adjustments in management's attitudes and programs were clearly in evidence two decades later. In the meantime, a number of other economic and environmental factors have contributed to the interest of business executives in good employee relations. One of these has been the change in the nation's work force with the sharp reduction of immigration after World War I and with the marked rise in the educational level of plant workers. Both developments appear to have wrought a permanent alteration in the American work group. Another significant factor has been the relative scarcity of labor, with high employment levels during the 1940's and 1950's. Whether labor will continue to enjoy such a seller's market in future decades is, of course, uncertain, but the relative scarcity seems likely to continue during the next decade for the reasons explained in Chapter 1. However, industry's recruiting, supervisory, and grievance-handling practices have been influenced by that scarcity, which has also helped to mold the cultural climate in America. Taking advantage of developments in the field of psychology, industry has increasingly stressed employee morale, job satisfaction, worker security, and understanding of the company through communication, persuasion, and participation.

During the 1930's and 1940's, labor and employee relations received increasing attention at higher levels of management. The staffs and programs of industrial relations departments absorbed a growing proportion of company budgets and labor costs, as new techniques were tried and the coverage of company benefits was extended to employees' dependents and even pensioners and their dependents.

Somewhat uncertain is the extent to which American management has accepted unions as a permanent feature of our business system. Obviously, a considerable section of industry has gone some distance in that direction by accepting the union shop, by abstaining from attempts at short-circuiting unions or at strike-breaking, and by signing long-term agreements and jointly administered benefit programs. Of course, some managements continue to challenge the existence of unions in their plants and seek to reduce their effectiveness by take-it-or-leave-it offers. Perhaps in the last few years a halt has occurred in the general movement toward increasing acceptance of unions by American management.[6] However, any anti-union efforts are more characteristic of legislatures and the national employers associations (the National Association of Manufacturers and the Chamber of Commerce of the United States) than they are of the bulk of American management at the plant or company level. It is significant, for instance, that, while the NAM continues to condemn all forms of union security, a very high percentage of the unionized companies represented on its directorate have agreements containing union-security clauses.[7] Practice seems to have disregarded national association pronouncements.

Maturing Union-Management Relations

As the parties accumulate experience with collective bargaining, their relationship usually becomes more stable and negotiations are likely to be more amiable and factual. A number of factors help to account for such a change. The longer they negotiate, the better they come to know and understand one another and, consequently, surprises are less frequent. Also collective bargaining tends to lead to common problem-solving and the establishment and use of joint machinery for such endeavors. Moreover, continued collective bargaining usually results in the settlement of some of the big issues that, at first, sharply divided union and management leaders, such as the grievance procedure, union security, noncontributory pensions, and supplementary unemployment benefits. Such advances often establish directions and institutional patterns that, to some extent, channel future developments and, therefore, have long-run consequences.

Long-term agreements and bargained benefit programs

are additional evidence of maturity in labor relations. Agreements covering three to five years imply continued dealings. Negotiated benefit arrangements strengthen the institutional position of a union by making the union a part of another area of worker interest, by adding new union functions that require staff experts, and by making the program dependent on the union even to the extent of joint administration.

Of course, the more technical and centralized negotiations become, the greater is the possibility of circumvention of the bargaining process. Collective bargaining has the important value of contributing to an understanding of the problems and perspectives of the other party. Insofar as that educational benefit is forestalled by a "deal" in advance of negotiations, which then become mere role-playing, collective bargaining has failed to perform one of its most important functions. Thus, certain types of maturity in labor-management relations can lead to real trouble in the future. Such restriction, even corruption, of collective bargaining is discussed in Chapter VI.

General Economic Conditions

High levels of employment, continually rising living standards, and more equal distribution of income have brought significant changes in the structure of our economy and in union programs. The long-run implications of full employment for the American labor movement need careful study.

Professor Sumner H. Slichter has pointed out that class lines in this country have become more blurred in recent years as the number of semi-skilled, white-collar, and technical jobs have expanded relative to unskilled employment, and as differences in family incomes have narrowed for such reasons as the compression of wage differentials, the wage-earning wife, and highly progressive tax rates. Growth in middle-class incomes and occupations, in his opinion, helps to explain both the decline in extreme views and class thinking and the dominance of moderation in American politics in recent years.[8]

Trade unions, as agents of worker protest and discontent, can hardly be expected to wax in an era of rising incomes, price-level stability, and full employment. In the midst of marked economic progress, general dissatisfaction is at a minimum. Under such conditions, workers' protest is likely to take mainly the form of plant grievances, which are individual or small-group complaints about particular local actions by management.

Prosperity poses some difficult problems for American unionism. Our labor movement is divisive in nature. The individual national unions are autonomous in policy determination and each is based on a specified jurisdiction. Autonomy and jurisdiction have played important roles in American trade-union history. Collective bargaining in this country is wholly sectional, and, in a period of high-level employment, sectional bargaining seems to pay off for the membership. At least the unions can claim credit for large negotiated increases, although economic conditions may have facilitated them.

Full employment, by diminishing concern for the general welfare, serves to strengthen centrifugal forces in a labor movement. Given the divisive characteristics of American unionism and the lack of class consciousness or a labor party to supply a cohesive influence, disunity in organized labor is likely to be particularly prominent in this country during prosperous periods. The AFL-CIO may not fragment during a further period of high-level employment but disintegrating tendencies have certainly not diminished in strength since the merger was consummated in December 1955.

Unless the business cycle has somehow been abolished, we shall experience future dips in employment. It is possible that some of them may be sufficiently deep and extended as to cause growing concern for the general welfare and to give rise to widespread discontent. Such a development would be likely to increase militancy and unity in our labor movement. Maintenance of high-level employment, on the other hand, is likely to continue to favor the centrifugal and divisive forces in American labor.

The Cultural Climate

The cultural atmosphere of the 1950's has not been an especially congenial one for protest agencies. These times have been dominated by a spirit of conformity, moderation, and middle-class values.[9] Left wing ideologies and movements have withered in this country. The Socialist Party is rapidly disappearing; liberal organizations have almost vanished from college campuses. The prevailing business creed of corporate management is confronted with few serious challenges.

In this era of suburban living and thinking, it seems increasingly more difficult to maintain a missionary zeal for the cause of the wage-earner, to preserve a sense of dedication to the ideals and traditions of organized labor. Of course, many union leaders struggle against the drift toward moderation and materialism. But the membership and some of the hierarchy are bound to become infected to some extent by the prevailing mood and current views.

Cultural climates, of course, do change. The spirit of these times undoubtedly is related to the economic conditions that have prevailed since World War II. To some extent it is perhaps a reaction to the radical changes made by the New Deal in the 1930's. There are cycles in intellectual climate as well as in more material things. Periods of experimentation and radical ventures are followed by a desire for consolidation and orderly existence. Change in the prevailing spirit one can expect, but it is doubtful, in the absence of marked change, such as serious economic depression, that radical ideas and radical movements will soon come into vogue.

In a sense, the cultural matrix of contentment and conformity matches the maturity in union-management relations. Both the climate and the relations seem part of a process of settling down to a stable, orderly existence.

Community Integration

In recent years, unions have branched out into numerous community activities. A conscious effort has been made to broaden union programs in order to integrate organized labor more closely with other elements in the community.

One phase of this effort has been the formation of Community Services Committees at the national and local levels. Under this AFL-CIO program, 110 labor representatives operate as full-time staff members of Community Chest and United Funds, and 60,000 representatives of organized labor serve on the committees or boards of welfare agencies, hospitals, scouts, schools, and other community organizations.[10] In addition, union members function as volunteer workers in the fund-raising, publicity, and administrative activities of various welfare agencies.

AFL-CIO encouragement of such labor participation is understandable in view of the fact that union members contribute to and use both the volunteer and public welfare agencies. Such activities on the part of unions have the advantage that they get credit for them and have an influence in policy determination.

In addition, participation with management at a high level in a non-conflict endeavor emphasizes common interests and increases the social recognition and respectability of unions and labor leaders. It reduces the feeling that organized labor is a group apart from the community, and increases the reliance of workers and the community upon unions. Undoubtedly, integration of unions into community activities is a moderating influence on union leadership.

Labor's community services program has the added advantage of providing "good causes" to absorb the missionary zeal in the membership. It may appeal to the idealism of youthful members, and help to gain acceptance for unions among women in the community.

The broader interests of organized labor extend into areas such as housing, education, civil rights, taxation, social insurance, and foreign affairs. In various ways, labor's community programs are associated with its programs for political education and political action.

Political Action

As already explained, the social climate in the 1950's has been less congenial to unions than it was in the 1930's. The transformation in public sentiment is evident in such legislation as the Taft-Hartley Act and "right-to-work" laws in eighteen states and also in the decisions of the National Labor Relations Board and the courts. The Senate investigations in 1955-1957 of abuses in negotiated welfare funds and of "improper practices in the labor and management field" are additional indications of political reaction to the exercise of power by organized labor.

Since World War II, political activity has absorbed an increasing share of union effort, and it is in this area that the organizing talent and aggressiveness of labor officials is becoming noteworthy. In part, organized labor has been forced to enter increasingly into politics in order to meet the challenge of unfavorable labor legislation and administration of such legislation. In addition, union leaders recognize that collective bargaining is unsuited for achieving certain broad objectives and that some of the gains of collective bargaining can be lost without the protection of favorable legislation. To date, union officials seem to have been more conscious of such matters and more anxious to have unions participate in political action than has been true of the bulk of the rank-and-file members.[11]

Significant and expanding political action by American unionism seems likely to continue far into the future. To some extent, the expansion in union political activity has been stimulated by factors that may disappear, such as the cold war or anti-union legislation, but many of the incentives for such action are likely to continue indefinitely. Of course, the younger leaders in former cio unions have tended to be the most militant politically and some of that aggressiveness may diminish with more experience and sophistication.

Some perspective on political activity by American unions may help in understanding the influence that this factor may have on future development of trade unionism in this country. Union political action is not new and is not nearly as radical in character as it has been at times during the past century and a half. For example, a "Working Men's Party" —the first known labor party in the world—flourished in New England, New York, Pennsylvania, and Ohio in the years from 1829 to 1832. Its program was certainly a radical one for the times.

In considering labor in politics one should bear in mind that government is the art of workable compromise among a diversity of interests. It involves some understanding of other elements in the community. By emphasizing a broad view and some responsibility for the interests of others, it often serves as a moderating influence. Abroad, in democratic nations such as England and Sweden, labor governments have probably, on balance, been restraining influences on the labor movements in those countries. Particularly if the temper of the times favors the *status quo,* political activity by unions is more likely to extend their integration into society than it is to increase their militancy.

This chapter has examined the effects of environmental

influences upon American unionism. The focus has been principally upon long-run developments and trends.

By way of conclusion it could be said that for unions the environment seems to have become less and less challenging and more and more comfortable. True, organized labor has faced some hostile employers and some adverse labor legislation, but in many areas of labor legislation (minimum wages, social insurance, and fair employment practices) small advances continued to be made. The hostile employers —mainly in the South, in small towns, and in small firms— have not, generally speaking, been expanding in number or importance.

Elsewhere unions have, so to speak, arrived, become partly integrated into the community, and found a fairly secure place in society. Union leaders have been seeking to broaden their sphere of operations but have not been pushing for radical changes. In a climate of moderation, suburban living, and material well-being, the leaders' standards for union success and the standards by which members judge unions seem to be approaching more closely to those applied to business concerns. More and more union leaders are to be found in plush offices, first-class hotels, and fine homes, living like prosperous businessmen.

Will the environment stimulate future militancy in American unionism by new challenges and the pressures of adversity? Is organized labor apt to expand in ways that will engender widespread hostility on the part of other elements in the society?

Projection of recent social trends would lead one to doubt either development. Legislation to correct abuses within the labor movement would not be likely to produce militant programs and much more aggressive top leadership. Nor are economic and social currents tending to stimulate rank-and-file militancy. On the contrary, life at both levels seems more conductive to comity than enmity, to industrial peace than to union-management strife. Significant expansion of labor organization into white-collar occupations, small firms, and small towns also seems highly unlikely over the next few years.

It would, of course, be foolhardy to project the present into the future, unchanged in content or in course. History reveals frequent environmental shifts, causing new challenges to established institutions. All one can say is that analysis of the recent past gives little reason to anticipate an environment that would be highly hostile to unionism in America. That conclusion seems valid even though the Select Committee of the Senate may continue to uncover unsavory facts about unions and a few more states may enact "right-to-work" laws that remain, for the most part, unenforced.

V. DYNAMIC FORCES IN AMERICAN UNIONISM

ORGANIZED LABOR IN AMERICA has its special, dynamic qualities. Unions are instruments for articulating and achieving the aspirations of industrial workers. As such, they service the needs of their clientele and help to generate and formulate new demands. Often the processes and pressures of worker representation, as explained in the preceding chapter, lead to enlarged horizons and additional activities.

Much of the expansionist drive in unions takes the form of new organization. Part of the business of labor organizations is to spread the faith by winning new converts. The gospel may be that of a CIO unionist, stemming from experience in the 1930's, or the bread-and-butter program of a craft-centered union, molded in the Gompers tradition. The American labor movement has been sufficiently comprehensive and elastic to encompass many varieties and mixtures of idealism and opportunism. Both the highly idealistic and the lowly practical can claim as their goal an improved status and a better life for the worker.

What are the wellsprings of healthy and vigorous unionism? What forces stimulate expansion and innovation? What factors tend to make unions unaggressive and conservative?

More systematic and searching study is necessary before confident answers can be supplied to those questions. All that can be attempted here is a preliminary examination of elements, such as internal pressures and rivalry, that tend to invigorate unions and to drive them on to new conquests.

On the opposite side, of course, are the factors that shift the balance from expansion to containment and that weaken a union's forward thrust.

Our discussion of union invigorating and enervating factors will, therefore, cover not only the missionary spirit and the role of competition but also the reduced opportunities for pioneering and the tendencies toward stagnation and unperturbed existence.

The Missionary Spirit

American unions have constituted part of a movement, designed to alter existing rights and privileges for the benefit of workers. As a vehicle for social change, organized labor in the United States has had its own folklore and songs, its traditions and martyrs. Union members are "brothers." They do not "scab" on one another, nor do they cross the picket lines of other unions. The "good" unionist is willing to sacrifice for the cause; unions open their treasuries to other unions suffering under the financial strain of a serious strike. And organized labor considers that its common interests extend internationally to workers in Canada, Europe, Latin America, and elsewhere.

A significant part of the motive power behind organized labor stems from personal dedication to its cause. Zeal for the cause of unionism is likely to be particularly prominent during the early stages of a union's development. Personal loyalty and devotion supply much of the volunteer work, so essential to the life of a union, especially at the local level. It is the "actives," mostly unpaid for their services, who constitute the grass roots of trade unionism. They account for much of a union's vitality and moral tone. And it is in their interest to preserve the democratic tradition of American unionism against centralizing encroachment in the name of efficient administration from the top.

The ethical aspects of trade unionism help to explain its

humanitarian aims and resistance to the corroding influence of material success.[1] A dedicated leadership is likely to strive not simply for wage increases but also for items like hospital and medical care, vesting rights to a pension, and other insurance protection extending beyond the employee's retirement from the bargaining unit and beyond the termination of his dues payments to the union. The importance of a missionary spirit is evident in the history of such unions as the Amalgamated Clothing Workers, the International Ladies' Garment Workers, and the United Automobile Workers. To a considerable extent these unions reflect the vision and crusading spirit of Sidney Hillman, David Dubinsky, and Walter Reuther.

The Role of Rivalry

Unions are subject to a variety of competitive pressures, both economic and political. Some types of competition are invigorating and serve to strengthen unions through constructive opposition and contests. Other types are destructive, draining a union's spirit and its resources with little hope of success. In this second category, for instance, are cases of employer opposition that prevent effective labor organization, or basic jurisdictional battles between two unions that become prolonged and bitter.

For unions, economic competition may take such forms as competition between union and nonunion areas producing the same commodity, competition between union and nonunion labor for employment in a locality, and competition of the members of different unions producing substitutable articles or services (i.e., coal miners and oil workers, or railroad workers and truck drivers). Generally speaking, such economic competition is less enlivening for unions than are certain types of political rivalry. Economic difficulties, of course, may lead to political differences.

Political competition centers around control, power, and

prestige. Within local and national unions it may take the form of ideological factionalism or personal rivalry for elective offices. Between national unions the competition may be for jurisdiction and membership, as evidenced by contests for certification by the National Labor Relations Board as sole bargaining agent. At the national level it may also be rivalry for prestige in the labor movement. One union leadership may seek to establish, through negotiated gains or breakthroughs, that it can outdo the leadership of rival unions in imaginative and skillful collective bargaining. Noteworthy during the past decade has been the rivalry between John Lewis (Mineworkers' president) and Walter Reuther (Autoworkers' president) and between Reuther and David McDonald (Steelworkers' president).

Absence of a two-party system (which exists only in the Typographical Union) handicaps any competitive struggle for power within a union. The in-group can discourage potential rivals for elective office through its control of patronage, official channels of communication, and judicial machinery such as the convention. Without a free press, an independent judiciary, and open election contests, democracy may lack the supports that are necessary for healthy functioning of the process.

Of course, employer opposition can provide some of the challenge and criticism of programs inherent in two-party contests. Skillful handling of grievances and negotiations of new contracts by a company or employers' association may reveal weaknesses in the union and its leadership. Strikes also may severely test leadership qualities and union strength; frequently they develop rivals for positions of power within unions.

As an opposition body, unionism may also be invigorated by unfavorable governmental action—legislation, administrative rulings, or court decisions. If the action is not too restrictive or damaging, and especially if it seems somewhat unfair, the reaction of the leadership and membership may have wholesome, energizing consequences. It is possible, for example, that the Taft-Hartley Act, on balance, has served to strengthen the labor movement by stimulating political activity and merger, although it has reduced the expansive powers of some weak unions.

Have the challenges to organized labor been decreasing in recent years so that well-established unions have lacked and will lack sufficient opposition to keep them in a vigorous, dynamic condition over the long run? Certainly that is a possibility. Employer opposition to unions, especially in large firms and urban areas, seems to have been decreasing during the past two decades. Nonunion competition has also diminished in many industries. The intensity of interunion rivalry has declined with no-raiding pacts, the AFL-CIO merger, and arrangements for settling jurisdictional disputes. Ideological conflict within the labor movement has been lessened with the decline of socialism and left wing influences. The settling-down process in the newer unions, along with increased size, more centralization of control, and the union shop and check-off of dues, have enabled the top leadership of many unions to become well entrenched and relatively secure.

For some unions, the spur of competition and the stimulus for emulation may already have become so blunted as to have portents for future union developments. In recent years, leaders of certain unions have had less pressure to pioneer—to set new patterns or achieve new breakthroughs—and less compulsion to follow patterns set by other unions. Of course, rank-and-file discontent sets limits to the laxity and indolence of a leadership. The extent to which both membership and leadership feel the force of compulsory comparison with gains made by other unions will vary with the circumstances. In any event, the stimulus of contrast and comparison assumes the existence of effective pattern-setting.

Declining Opportunity for Innovation

Collective bargaining in the United States has been characterized by new and extraordinary developments. All kinds of subjects, from seniority to medical care and the guaranteed wage, have been brought within the orbit of union-management negotiations. So ambitious has American unionism been to expand the area of its influence and authority that employers have complained loudly and often about unions invading management prerogatives and seeking to control production, prices, and even industrial location.

Organized labor in America has appeared more enterprising than unionism in Western Europe for a variety of reasons. The pioneering atmosphere of this country has meant less of the restraint of tradition upon experimentation in collective bargaining. Wide industrial diversity and rapidity of change in our economy have caused considerable variation and frequency of adjustment. Company-by-company bargaining (in contrast to the dominant practice of employer-association bargaining abroad) has permitted more stress on the ability of individual firms to pay and to experiment. Moreover, in this country collective bargaining has proved more rewarding than legislative action, whereas abroad the opposite has often been true—new gains have been achieved more easily via the legislative route than through negotiations with tightly organized employers' associations.

As unions accumulate experience with collective bargaining the question arises whether the range of its possibilities becomes progressively restricted. Do unions in the early years of bargaining exploit so many of the opportunities that the scope for pioneering is curtailed as union-management relations mature? Some evidence seems to point toward an affirmative answer to that question.

Labor organization grows out of worker discontent and protest. Immediately after the unionization of a firm, the parties have many matters that call for attention and correction. The union seeks to establish new rights, rules, and procedures intended to eliminate alleged favoritism, inequities, and other grievances. For both sides the early years represent a trial period, in which new relationships and other innovations are developed. As time passes many of the causes of the union's complaints are eliminated; some of its goals are at least partially achieved. Employment practices and conditions are more satisfactory, management becomes more human-relations minded, and the employees enjoy more income security.

Looked at broadly, the gap between the plant and the office has been narrowed as the rights and privileges of production workers have been brought into closer alignment with those of staff and white-collar employees. As pointed out in the preceding chapter, plant employees now enjoy more respect and respectful treatment. For them the taint of social inferiority has been partly removed by such means as paid vacations, sick and reporting pay, and guaranteed wages. Full employment has lent a helping hand, but unions themselves have been instrumental in directing gains into those non-wage channels.

More and better "fringe benefits" have not, of course, reduced the workers' drive for improved living standards, for which American labor is noted. But the point is that past expansions in the scope of bargaining may have diminished the number of new outlets for that drive so that increasingly it is contained within well worn channels. In other words, past union conquests may have curtailed the possibilities for future pioneering—at least by means of collective bargaining.

Unions as "Sleepy Monopolies"

Economic theorists, assessing the bargaining power of unions, have been prone to assume that they would press unrelentingly for wages as high as "the traffic would bear," that a union's main aim is and has to be the maximum economic gain for its membership.[2] Some labor economists, on the other hand, have concluded that most top leaders of unions function as "lazy monopolists," who are "more likely to secure the minimum they require for political purposes than the maximum they could obtain for economic reasons."[3]

Which view is valid? Are union leaders intent upon exploiting the full bargaining power of their organizations or are they more interested in organizational security and in leadership stability and convenience?

Those who believe that labor organizations tend to be "moderate monopolies" use in support of that position an analysis of unions as institutions and the statistics of wage experience. Their institutional analysis includes an examination of union leadership, which defines and applies the organizational objective.

A number of institutional factors help to explain why particular unions are less aggressive than might be assumed on theoretical grounds. In the first place, there is no single test of union success equivalent to net profit for business firms. Wages are only one element in package settlements and elaborate agreements. Membership satisfaction is rather intangible, and differences in industrial and other conditions make it difficult to compare the achievements of one union with those of another union or to determine that the results would have been better for the membership under another leadership. For the leadership, election and reelection to office is the principal test of success. Given considerable inertia, if not apathy, among the membership of many unions, the size of relative economic gains for the membership may be no more important for winning elections than the development of a political machine and the achievement of political balance and control. Generally unions contain within their membership conflicting and competitive interests that must be compromised and balanced in order to preserve the integrity and well-being of the institution itself.

Second, certain institutional arrangements serve to reduce the pressures on union leaders to deliver large economic gains. For example, once a union is certified by the National Labor Relations Board it enjoys sole bargaining rights for the certification period and, with a union-shop contract, the union has at least a temporary assurance of dues income regardless of shifts in membership satisfaction.

Third, the top leadership in a union usually has an interest in settling problems and maintaining peaceful relations with employers. Strikes create risks for the union and for its leadership. Mutual accommodation and workable compromises tend to reduce the risks on both sides; good relations may be more valuable to a union than maximum exploitation of its bargaining power.

Fourth, union leaders often are willing to sacrifice potential economic gains for ease and convenience of administration. For instance, they generally favor industry-wide (multiple-employer) bargaining, although that arrangement may strengthen the bargaining power of the employers and, by replacing differentiated company wage levels with a uniform industry wage scale, may eliminate the possibility of the union "charging" each employer according to his ability to pay.

Without sales competition or some other objective test of success, unions may lack an effective check on administrative inefficiency. However, the nature of negotiations is such that the leadership can claim credit for past wage gains that it negotiated, even though they might have occurred in the absence of the union. The dramatic character of negotiated increases lends credence to claims of personal or institutional credit.

Statistics of wage developments in different industries during the past half century seem to indicate little consistent relationship between labor organization and relative increase in wages. Generally speaking, wage increases have been about as great percentage-wise in nonunion and slightly-organized lines as in highly unionized industries. Only in the early years of organization, when the unions are expanding rapidly as in mass-production industries in the mid-1930's, does it appear that wages have risen more rapidly in the well organized sectors of the economy.[4] That fact, plus the absence of any pulling apart of the wage structure in a way that would correspond to the bargaining power of labor in different lines,[5] seems to confirm the contention that unions do not behave like aggressive monopolies—at least after they settle down and the leadership becomes entrenched. The stability in the share of the national income received by labor since 1929, despite marked changes in labor organization, also tends to confirm the conclusion that unions in time may become somewhat "sleepy monopolies."[6]

That conclusion might perhaps have to be qualified slightly if allowance were made for non-wage gains in the form of various benefit programs. It is interesting to observe, however, that the pioneers in negotiated benefits in the 1920's, like the Amalgamated Clothing Workers and the International Ladies' Garment Workers, have been most conservative in their demands and behavior in the 1940's and 1950's. Both unions have been practically strike free since World War II and have foregone wage increases for periods of two or three years.

It is not surprising that a social institution such as a union should change with shifts in the needs of the membership and with institutional accommodation and leadership stability. That the pressures and compulsions on the leadership decline somewhat as a union matures does not, of course, mean that it loses all of its dynamism and drive. New challenges may arise at any time to end any imperceptible drift toward unperturbed existence.

To sum up the observations in this chapter, unions start out as dynamic forces for industrial change. A missionary zeal contributes to organizational expansion. Pressures for improvements lead to innovations. There is a fairly urgent demand by the membership and leadership for "more"—the better life economically, socially, and politically.

As the union achieves many of its objectives and the leadership matures, some of the potential opportunities are fairly well exploited and the pressures of internal political rivalry are reduced. The union takes on many of the attributes of other large and well-established organizations.

The dynamic force of worker discontent remains. The American worker continually presses for improved living and working standards, but his drive for change is directed more and more into well-worn channels.

Compared with the formative years, union leadership is generally in a position to exercise greater control, and to enjoy more of the rewards of union success and personal achievement. The next chapter examines in some detail the tendency for idealistic zeal and moral standards to change in the settling-down process.

VI. CORRUPTING INFLUENCES IN
AMERICAN UNIONISM

ORGANIZED LABOR is subject to the corrupting factors present in the American environment. The union ideal of personal sacrifice to promote the workers' cause is difficult to preserve untarnished in a materialistic civilization, dominated by business values and standards of conduct and blessed with increasingly luxurious living.

The corrupting influences to which union officials may succumb take many and subtle forms. Often it is difficult to draw a clear distinction between justified and unjustified personal gain of labor leaders or between valid application and abuse of their power. Involved are such questions as the proper use of union monies (including expense accounts and welfare funds), the distribution and receipt of favors and union patronage, the use of questionable means to achieve organizational aims, and the levy of compulsory payments of different kinds, ranging from union assessments and fines to various forms of extortion.

The issue of corruption leads directly to the theory of American unionism. Union ideals provide internal protections against moral decay. For the most part, the aims of American unionism have been centered on practical, bread-and-butter issues. Stress has been placed on collective bargaining and, structurally, loose national and state federations have permitted sectional groups to pursue their own self-interests with few cohesive pressures, ethical or otherwise, exerted by the union centers. That at least was true prior to the adoption of a code of ethical practice and a code of union democratic processes by the AFL-CIO in May 1957. In contrast, European unionism has been class-conscious and dominated by political and social philosophies, particularly socialism. To a considerable degree, the mission and class character of European unionism have supplied safeguards against exploitation of unions for personal profit by their officials. For a number of decades, European observers have commented about the remarkable degree of outright corruption in American unionism, from which their own labor organizations have been largely exempt.[1]

With respect to corruption and racketeering, the contrast between Canadian unionism and organized labor in this country has been noteworthy. Canadian unions have been almost completely free from corruption and scandals. A number of factors help to explain this difference between countries with common national unions—most large American unions have Canadian affiliates. In Canada, the British pattern of law observance and enforcement early became traditional, Canada has not been plagued by corrupt local political machines, and she did not suffer from the lawlessness of our prohibition and post-prohibition eras. Also, the underlying philosophy of unionism in Canada seems more Spartan, if not more inspirational, and the environment presents fewer temptations.[2]

Whether corrupting influences in organized labor in America have been increasing with environmental changes and as unions have grown in size and power, is difficult to determine. Some writers have stressed that the opportunities and temptations for personal enrichment of officials at the workers' expense have grown with the increase in the power of unions, with the expanding volume of funds under union control, and with the changing living standards of union hierarchs.[3] Also, it is claimed that the centralization of union control and the entrenchment of top labor leaders afford greater latitude of action to the officialdom and reduce the checks on waste and improper activities.

Obviously, whether corruption has experienced a relative increase in American unionism, and if so why, are important questions in any study of the evolution of organized labor in America. Occasional investigations of corrupt or improper practices in unions and in union-management relations, such as those of the Select (McClellan) Committee of the United States Senate in 1957, are helpful in understanding the factors that contribute to corruption in unions but they may be of little assistance in determining whether such corruption has or has not increased in recent decades. Indeed, mistaken notions about trends can easily be created by the timing and thoroughness of any particular exposé, or by the extent of both awareness of the problem and attempts at remedial action.

Failing a systematic study of racketeering in unions that covers at least a decade, it is not possible definitely to determine whether the corrupting influences within American unionism have been waxing or waning. One can, however, analyze the factors and developments that contribute to corruption in union affairs and by that means arrive at some understanding of underlying forces. Instead of stress on single "horrible" examples, such an analysis examines developments within American unions and their environment that affect the character of our labor organizations and their leadership.

In considering labor racketeering—the use of union position or control over labor in order to extort money for personal advantage—it is necessary to recognize that such extortion has generally been most prevalent in local-market types of industry such as building construction and service, longshoring, amusement, local transport, and produce markets. The absence of outside competition permits the burdens of racketeering to be levied upon local business without any need to worry about injury to it in competition with firms located elsewhere. And the concentration of power to call strikes and allocate employment in the hands of a local union official, as in the case of the business agent in building construction, facilitates shake-downs, kickbacks, and other iniquitous action.

In this chapter, the factors that contribute to corrupt activities in unions will be analyzed under three headings: erosion of union ideals, decay of union democracy, and union methods and power. Following such an analysis, possible future developments will be considered.

Erosion of Union Ideals

Particularly in its early stages, trade unionism assumes the character of a crusade, with high ideals, strong moral precepts, and a missionary zeal, which generates self-sacrifice, creates unity through a common feeling, and helps to preserve the integrity of the organization. Understandably, it is difficult to maintain the militancy and idealism of the formative years. As the union settles down to a more mundane and routine existence, the scale of values of leaders and members shifts and corroding influences are prone to seep in.

The moral climate in the community is one such influence. In this country, economic gain is a prime measure of success, and the morals of the market place significantly affect our cultural standards. True, our commercial codes of morality are modified and restricted by standards of social, professional, and even political ethics. But a considerable section of the American public continues to admire the clever fellow who "makes a fast buck" by cutting corners and the "fixer" who "works" his connections or buys his way out of difficulties.

The situation with respect to levels of morality is, of course, mixed. Generally speaking, standards of public conduct have probably improved in America over the past century. At least some evidence appears to support the view that "Both individual and public moral standards seem to have been slowly rising in all particulars that can be measured."[4] However, moral advance has been subject to setbacks during postwar or inflationary periods, and it has been less evident in certain industries and some local governments than in others.

The ethics of American business and politics, of course, have a direct influence on labor organizations and leaders, for union activities center on industry and government. If businessmen and politicians are making money in questionable ways, and "getting away with it," union leaders may be tempted to do likewise. The temptation may be particularly strong when union leaders are handling large sums of money and the sense of moral dedication has decreased within the organization.

Another factor tending to reduce the effectiveness of union idealism has been the rising living standards and status of the membership. Fervor for the workers' cause may be more difficult to maintain when members are enjoying a greatly improved level of material well-being and attendance at union meetings suffers from the attractiveness of such living standards.

Acquisitive impulses also are stimulated by the changing pattern of life of the labor leader. Nowadays the president of a national union is the manager of a well-established enterprise, which is responsible for numerous solid benefits embodied in enforceable contracts. In unions with 50,000 or more members, his duties, salary, office, and expense account approach those of the executive head of a medium-sized firm. For instance, the top dozen salaries of union presidents ranged from $33,000 to $60,000 in 1957; the average salary of the presidents of the 15 largest unions, having a quarter of a million to one and a half million members was over $30,000 a year.[5] In addition, some union leaders charge large sums to their official expense accounts, because they stay at the best hotels, enjoy fine food and drink, and spend rather lavishly on "entertainment."[6] Many of them devote considerable time to investments of various sorts, including personal stock and property holdings, while their families seek to fulfill upper middle-class aspirations. Under those circumstances, the way of life of some union leaders may not be significantly different from that enjoyed by executives in business and other types of enterprise.

The metamorphosis in the outlook and philosophy of union presidents over the past two decades is part of the evolutionary process in American unionism. The days of significant self-sacrifice for the cause have largely disappeared; the temptations to use the union for purposes of personal gain seem to have increased, at least in some unions. In view of the developments within unions and society at large, it seems doubtful that the old union virtues will generally regain their earlier power to combat corrupting influences.

Decay of Union Democracy

In addition to standards of moral conduct, unions rely on democratic processes to help prevent corruption and improper activities. Democratic controls, including discussion, disclosure, and membership approval by majority vote, are assumed to be particularly effective at the local level, where the units are not too large and the members are well acquainted with one another. An additional check at the local level is the supervision exercised by the national over the activities and finances of its locals.

In unions in some local-market lines, such as the building trades, local democratic control may be weakened by the centering of considerable power in the hands of a business agent. In other unions, local democratic checks may be rendered less effective by an increasing centralization of functions and control in the national headquarters. No higher body actually supervises or approves the activities and finances of the national union. Sovereignty of the national union means that the AFL-CIO exercises only the most general moral influence, with a threat of expulsion of an affiliate found to be corrupt, Communist-dominated, or otherwise in violation of the constitution of the top federation.

The national union is much more likely to be controlled by a personal political machine than is true of the locals. Election contests and turnover of officers are generally far more frequent in locals than at the national level. The national administration of a union usually has many sources of power and control that enable it to remain in office unchallenged. The president has considerable patronage to dispense; he generally appoints, in some cases subject to approval by the union's executive board, the national union's representatives, the organizers, and staff personnel. During the past two decades there has actually been a tendency to give union presidents appointive power unrestricted by executive board approval. Heads of most European unions do not enjoy anything like the patronage power of our union presidents.[7]

The officialdom tends to behave like a government ruling over the membership and entrusted with the union's destiny. The president and his appointees generally control the lines of communication within the union, including the union's newspaper or magazine. The national's administration manages the convention, which serves as both the 'legislature and supreme court in most national unions. The president or the national headquarters also can withdraw local charters, appoint trustees to take over the affairs of a local, and control the expenditure of funds of the national union, including strike funds. By such means, officials can help to perpetuate themselves in office and penalize critics of their leadership. In addition, as a union shakes down, as the officers become entrenched, and as the most active members congeal into "one team," a tendency exists for union conventions to grant increasing powers and authority to the president and the executive board. The corrupting influence of additional concentration of power within unions may be subtle but it is detectable from a reading of successive convention proceedings of particular unions and from informal conversations with persons in subordinate positions in those organizations.

Seldom is the head of a national union challenged in his use of union funds. There are a number of reasons why George Berry (late president of the Printing Pressmen), Joseph P. Ryan (ex-president of the International Longshoremen's Association), or Dave Beck (ex-president of the Teamsters) were able to use the union for personal profit with no condemnation from other top officials within the union. One has to bear in mind that national unions are practically all one-party organizations. With the pressure that exists in favor of unity and the belief that factions in a union weaken its effectiveness and border on disloyalty, any organized criticism of an entrenched leadership from within the union is risky and requires considerable courage. Furthermore, union advancement via election is restricted to that one union; mobility is upward through the hierarchy, subject to the rewards and penalties of the ruling administration.

A national administration has at hand various sanctions. In addition to patronage and promotion within the union, it can levy fines and assessments and even expel a person from membership for such reasons as "insubordination," "conduct unbecoming a union member," or "slander" of an official. Such powers are especially significant where unions hold exclusive bargaining rights, where the union shop is widely established in the industry or occupation, and where union mobility is within the single union and not from one national union to another.

Other factors may tend to reduce the effectiveness of democratic checks within unions. They include the increased size of national unions and bargaining units, the development of more layers in the union hierarchy, and growth in rank-and-file non-participation in union meetings and activities. Where such developments occur, they help to expand any gap in viewpoint between the top and the bottom of the union pyramid. The life of national officials tends to be distinct from that of the rank-and-file, and headquarters officials may come to assume that they are experts who know best how to run the union and to negotiate agreements.

Personal rule, which is the antithesis of democracy, encourages deals (secret understandings in advance or in place of negotiations) between management and union officials. The "deal," which is a fairly well known phenomenon in American trade union history, is a form of corruption practically unknown to British or Scandinavian unionism—partly because of differences in moral and living standards among union officials here and abroad, but also because negotiations in England are more likely to be team operations and in Scandinavia to be subject to rank-and-file influence and control. To the extent that collective bargaining is short-circuited by a side deal, concealed by the subterfuge of role-playing, the process is really corrupted into a form of collusion, which may lead to some subtle means of personal "payoff" to the union official involved.

Often, of course, it is difficult to distinguish between genuine and collusive collective bargaining. Take the case of the United Mine Workers, which for decades John L. Lewis has ruled as a "benevolent despot," filling most of its executive board and district posts with personal appointees on the grounds that union "efficiency" is more important than union democracy. As indicated in Chapter III, Lewis and an executive of the Bituminous Coal Operators' Association made new agreements secretly without the use of negotiating committees during the period 1952 to 1958. Edward G. Fox, B.C.O.A. executive, explained in a speech at the end of 1956 that, while some may "feel that the present method of arriving at new contract terms could not be properly defined as negotiations," he "emphatically" believes it is; it has had the advantage of settlements without the threat of a strike deadline and has resulted in the union joining the operators "without reservation in all our efforts to combat the influence of competitive fuels, government interference, and unreasonable safety regulations."[8]

Some may consider such "businesslike dealing" and collaborative activities to be an advanced stage in collective bargaining and, therefore, evidence of maturity in union-management relations. Any such drift toward centralization of power and authority is, however, an indication of some atrophy of the democratic and bargaining processes. And a weakening of popular control and democratic checks within a union enhances the opportunities and temptations to use power for corrupt purposes.

Union Methods and Power

When unions are still struggling for their existence and security, they are likely to be headed by individuals who are not too squeamish about the means they employ to obtain their objectives. Some "labor statesmen," early in their careers, condoned the use of strong-arm methods and industrial sabotage. And even in recent years, it is not unusual for unions to violate the law by such means as mass picketing and roughing-up persons who oppose union policies.

In a few extreme cases, criminal elements in society have gained temporary control of union locals and have used them as a means of extorting money from employees, union members, and independent businessmen. When a union uses thugs to gain its ends, it opens itself to capture by racketeers.

A union's normal activities often involve the threat to use

pressure and power either against employers or in politics. As organized labor has gained in economic and political strength, its threats of punishment become more potent. The strike aims at inflicting economic damage. In politics, unions resort to lobbying, campaign contributions, and other political activities in order to obtain favorable treatment by government, including the police and the courts.

Union leaders are accustomed to the use of the threat of force and money to win their objectives. Their approval or disapproval of an employer's proposal may mean much to him in terms of money cost; their favor can, in some cases, represent significant economic advantages. Consequently, it has been possible for officials in a few unions to benefit personally from employer contributions to testimonial dinners and from gifts of one sort or another. In such cases, union power is for all practical purposes used to extort funds for items that may include a Cadillac car, a house, or a cash sum of as much as $10,000 to $60,000.[9]

As unions settle down and achieve security, the use of strong-arm methods tends to decline. Whether the more or less subtle use of union power for the personal profit of union officials similarly has been declining is, however, somewhat doubtful. Judging from scattered evidence, power is still a corrupting factor, especially in unions in local-market types of business.

The McClellan Committee received during the first half of 1957 a large volume of letters from union members charging misuse of union funds, sell-outs to management, racketeering, and local-union dictatorship maintained by various undemocratic methods, including trustees and gangster tactics.[10] Although more complaints were lodged against the Teamsters than any other union, many others were also named. If such widespread allegations have factual support, corruption of one kind or another is fairly prevalent in a significant section of organized labor in this country.

And what about the future? Will corruption in unions be reduced by measures recently taken—the AFL-CIO codes on democratic practices and financial practices of unions and the exposures of improper practices by the Select Committee of the United States Senate? Will it be curtailed by prospective legislative measures to safeguard union funds and to prevent financial abuses?

Only time can tell. However, many of the environmental and institutional factors that have contributed to corruption within American unions seem likely to continue to operate much as they have during the past decade. They are both pervasive and deep-seated. Consequently, vigorous and unremitting efforts will be required if some lasting reduction is to be effected in the acquisitive activities of union officials, pursued at the expense of their organizations and the membership.

VII. EXPERIENCE IN BRITAIN
AND SWEDEN

ALTHOUGH THIS STUDY is centered on American unionism, a brief examination of the development of the English and Swedish labor movements can be helpful for comparative purposes.

Organized labor in those countries has had a long and uninterrupted history. In some respects, their union-management relations are in a more mature stage of development than ours. It is even claimed that we are following in their footsteps, with a couple of decades' lag, according to some assumed pattern of evolution in labor relations.

An investigation of unionism in Great Britian and Sweden, however, reveals that there is no rigid pattern of evolution that applies internationally. Some of the same general tendencies have been present within the labor movements of a number of countries. But these tendencies may be promoted or retarded by institutional and other conditions in particular nations. The mores, ideology, and characteristics of the people may make considerable difference with respect to such matters as corruption of officials, the effectiveness of democratic and competitive checks, and interunion rivalry.

In this chapter, first British and then Swedish unionism will be considered from the viewpoint of evolutionary changes and trends. Since the focus is on major developments within trade unionism, no systematic treatment of the factual background—institutional, historical, and governmental—in each country will be presented.[1]

[73]

The Ageing of British Unionism

Three or four decades ago the English labor movement still had a number of youthful characteristics—considerable ruggedness and militancy, significant rivalry between and within unions, and severe strikes. Both sides tended to take a strong stand. Their combativeness reached a climax in the General Strike of 1926.

That sobering, almost frightening, experience served to convince both British labor and management of the need for a new approach to their industrial relations problems. Emphasis was placed on more joint machinery and on workable compromise. Many more joint industrial councils were established, teamwork and responsibility were stressed, and a downward trend in the strike statistics set in. British unions became somewhat "tame" by American standards.

Top union leadership has also "matured." The empire builders have been succeeded by second and third generation leadership. The General Council of the Trades Union Congress (the national federation) has tended to become a select circle of "labor statesmen," who have established a convention of viewing issues in terms of the whole labor movement and even the nation. Three factors have helped to broaden the viewpoint of British labor leaders: the holding of high governmental positions during World War II, their connections with the Labour Party, and the practice of bestowing titles on them and appointing them late in life to management positions in nationalized industries.[2]

As perspectives at top levels have enlarged, the gap between high union officials and the rank-and-file has tended to widen. Full employment and continuing price inflation during the postwar period have accentuated that condition. The General Council of the TUC has at times (as 1948-1950) taken a position in favor of wage restraint, which to the membership may seem an unnatural, if not incomprehensible, program for a union center to adopt.

Industrial developments have also served to separate high union officials from the general membership. More and more functions and powers have been centralized in the national union headquarters under national collective bargaining and with widespread use of national joint councils. National negotiations are remote from the rank-and-file and from local officials of the union, who do not participate in them, even as observers. Nor are they likely to be kept well informed of the discussions that occur in the privacy of the three or four negotiating sessions. And the negotiating machinery, so well developed at the national level, is weak at the plant level. In fact, historically in Britain, negotiations usually began at the district level before moving up to a national basis, so that, for the most part, an effective unit for bargaining is lacking at the plant level. So jealous are the national unions and employer associations of their power and control that they generally oppose the establishment of any new arrangements at the plant level.

Both the structure of bargaining and the negotiating methods have become traditional. In fact, the bargaining procedure follows a pattern that is practically uniform regardless of the industry or the unions involved. Industrial relations in Britain have developed such rigidity in method and mentality that innovations are practically precluded, and the structure has stabilized with weaknesses at the local level and narrow official channels of communication. As is the case in other countries and social institutions, British unionism suffers from the limitations imposed by historical accidents and vested interests.

In one respect, however, the top British labor leaders are closer to their membership than are their American counterparts. Their incomes and levels of living are not much above those of the men at the bench. They and their families remain part of the working class both in mode of life and in type of residence. The highest union salary in 1955 was the equiva-

lent of $5,600 a year; the general secretary (the full-time offi-
cial usually drawing the largest salary) of the Amalgamated
Engineering Union—a semi-industrial union with 800,000
members centered on skilled mechanics—was paid but about
$56 a week in 1956, which was only three-quarters as much
as the maintenance engineer was to receive in the new TUC
building in London.

Corruption in the form of shakedowns, misuse of union
funds for personal profit, or side-door deals, are practically
unknown in Britain. Such factors as class loyalty, the egali-
tarian ideals of socialism, and social restraints on conspicuous
consumption serve as curbs on acquisitive inclinations. And,
although union leaders through frequent meetings may come
to know employer representatives well, sell-outs or bribes
have been conspicuous by their absence from the union scene.
Apparently there is no need for the TUC to have an ethical
practices committee.

British unions during recent decades have experienced a
trend in the direction of centralization and administrative
efficiency at the expense of democratic control. As already explained, the gap between the top leadership and the rank-
and-file has been widening since the 1930's. Other factors
have also weakened democratic checks. In many unions the
control of the national executive council and the general
secretary has expanded. Except in a few unions with periodic
elections, the general secretaries practically have tenure of
office until retirement, and members of a union's executive
council can usually remain on it as long as they wish.[3] In
many unions, promotion is controlled by the executive council, through written and oral tests given to candidates for an
opening. Indeed, most union officials oppose arrangements
for periodic reelection of officers on the grounds that elections
promote irresponsibility and, with only a minority of the
membership participating, permit the communists to win
offices out of all proportion to their numbers in the ranks of

[76]

the union. Generally speaking, of course, membership apathy enhances control by the union's top officials.

True, the general secretaries of British unions do not have the personal patronage or the personal authority over locals and policies that are enjoyed by the presidents of many American unions. However, the general secretaries do develop control over channels of communication within the union and that, along with the executive council's control over promotion, may enable the national headquarters to squash all efforts at opposition to official policies. That has been the case, for example, in the two largest unions (Transport and General Workers with 1,300,000 members and the General and Municipal Workers with over 800,000 members) and in the Iron and Steel Trades Confederation (116,000 members). Also, the headquarters, with some notable exceptions,[4] generally are able to control the national conventions, which, as in this country, serve as the top legislative and judicial bodies of British unions. In other words, control from the top (the council and the general secretary) in most British unions seems to be fully as firm as is the case in the United States.

Unions in Great Britain have become stable and secure. With little expansion through organization, the invigorating effects of new growth are largely absent. Leadership rivalry and interunion competition have declined significantly during the past three or four decades, primarily because almost all negotiations now are on a multi-union basis, because the labor movement has fostered a cult of teamwork, and because public opinion frowns on unconventional forms of individual aggressiveness or selfishness. With no challenge to union security, labor leaders have tended to become tradition-bound, rather conservative, and adverse to the risk of attempting new ideas and programs. Perhaps both the fact that their labor problems were not solved by the nationalization of a number of industries after World War II, and the lack of marked success with the postwar program of union-management "joint consultation," have helped to make trade union leaders less venturesome. The chief type of competition or rivalry has been provided by communists within the labor movement, who have captured some of the top offices in a few unions, mostly those that hold periodic elections and have a high proportion of skilled craftsmen among their membership. Such factors as skill dilution and compression of wage differentials seem to have made the skilled workers relatively restless and discontented.

Labor protest and militancy have tended to be greater in the rank-and-file than up the line in the union pyramid. The problems that arise at the shop level—automation, skill dilution, layoffs, etc.—provide the dynamic forces to expand the scope of bargaining into new areas. For the most part, national negotiations deal only with wages, hours, holidays, and vacations; benefits, seniority, and similar items are generally not included in national agreements. Often wages are the sole subject of agreements from one year to the next, which means, of course, that national bargaining is of limited use in solving plant problems. Yet, as already explained, the national headquarters resists efforts by shop stewards' committees to act as a local industrial union, because they are composed of members of different unions and are beyond the control of a single labor organization.

That greater pressure and protest have existed at the local than at the national level seems to be indicated by the increasing significance of "unofficial strikes" locally during the past decade and by the fact that the gap between actual earnings and nationally negotiated rates expanded almost continually from 1938 to 1955.[5] It has been calculated that one-fifth of the increase in hourly earnings during that sixteen-year period is accounted for by the excess paid by employers, either on their own initiative or as a result of local bargaining, in such forms as "plus payments," piece rates above the nationally negotiated figures, or a loosening of production standards under incentive systems of payment.[6] It would seem either that bargaining at the national level has not pushed wages up as much as the full-employment, inflationary conditions would warrant or that bargaining power is sufficient at the local level to gain greater increases on the basis of ability to pay.

Although unofficial strikes have tended to increase, the trend in total man-days of time lost from labor disputes relative to total employment has been downward in Britain since 1926. For half a century there has been no industry-wide strike in steel in England. As the lockout has practically vanished and the strike weapon has atrophied until the relative strike loss in Britain is but one-half that in this country for the past two decades, resort to arbitration to settle disputes has become more frequent.[7] With about one-quarter of the products of British industry sold in foreign markets, English unionists must, of course, be more concerned than American labor leaders with the effects of strikes on the nation's markets and balance of payments.

To conclude, the main developments in British unionism since 1926 may be summarized as: less militancy, less rivalry, less innovation, a broader view at the top, more centralization, some loss of vitality at the local level, and a greater gap between top officials and the rank-and-file. These add up to some loss of dynamic qualities as the British unions have settled in and settled down.

Swedish Unionism: Vigorous Maturity

In the 1920's, industrial relations in Sweden were characterized by militancy and hostility. The heads of the union and employer federations (LO and SAF) were distant toward one another and communicated only by formal letters. The national union officials viewed employers as inherent opponents in a basic conflict of interests. Also, the national unions operated quite autonomously and occasionally found themselves fighting one another.

No one event, such as England's General Strike of 1926, transformed relations to a more friendly basis in Sweden. Rather it was a series of developments. The labor party—the Social Democrats—became the government in 1932, and alone or as the most important partner in coalitions, has been in power almost continuously for 25 years. In 1936 a new president of the union center (LO) was selected, who changed its policies. The LO became much more active: arranging conferences on wages and the economic situation, acquiring more influence over its affiliated national unions, taking part in governmental affairs, and working cooperatively with SAF. At first this interventionist program met considerable opposition from some national union leaders on the grounds that centralization would weaken the locals and the national unions would lose their "souls," but gradually the opposition was overcome by discussion and experience. World War II also served to increase centralization both within individual unions and in the hands of the LO. The top federations moved closer together in negotiating escalator wage agreements to apply to all of their affiliates.[8]

⸱ As an outgrowth of mutual confidence and improved relations, the central federations (LO and SAF) have negotiated a series of "framework" agreements, which apply in a particular industry only when ratified by the national union and employers' association directly concerned. These LO-SAF agreements have served to expand the scope of bargaining and to establish much joint machinery. They are the pioneering element in collective bargaining in Sweden and the means by which activities are brought under the control of the top federations and the national organizations. In 1938, LO and SAF adopted a "Basic Agreement" to protect workers against unfair discharge and third parties against injury in disputes; it established a bipartisan Labor Market Board to hear cases and make recommendations regarding those matters. In 1942, a LO-SAF agreement on workers' safety led to the establishment of a Joint Committee for Workers' Protection; a 1944 agreement for the promotion of occupational training resulted in a bipartisan Vocational and Guidance Council; an agreement concerning works councils in 1946 promoted the setting up of some 3,500 local joint production committees; a 1948 agreement concerning time-and-motion studies has as top disputes' settlement agency a joint Time-and-Motion Study Board; and, in 1951, a joint Labor Market Council for Women's Questions was established to deal with sex differentials in wages and with other aspects of female employment. As some of these agreements indicate, Swedish unions have come to accept certain management techniques and even parts of management's philosophy.

Efforts at wage restraint are a further indication of the reasoned and public-spirited attitude of LO officials, of members of LO's Representative Body, and of its Wage Policy Council, which is composed of a few leaders from affiliated national unions. For the years 1948 and 1949, LO asked all of its affiliated unions to extend their annual agreements with no change in wage scales, which was done. For 1953 and 1954, LO also recommended against across-the-board increases, restricting wage raises to special cases and groups. Master agreements for the years 1952 and 1956 were negotiated by LO-SAF, providing general increases of roughly 9 and 4 per cent respectively. The purpose of all of these centrally-set limits to wage advance was to combat price inflation. Another objective was to improve Sweden's competitive position in world markets.[9] Like the English, Swedish unions are especially aware of the effects of their actions on exports and the nation's balance of payments.

Any assumption that the national unions submit readily to central control of wages by LO would, however, be unwarranted. In the first place, the individual unions participate in the formulation of LO wage policy, and in some postwar years have opposed any central agreement on wages. Secondly, some individual unions have made strong efforts to exceed the LO-SAF limits during years of master agreements. That, for example, was true of the Paper Workers Union in 1952, when LO had to threaten to withdraw all moral and financial support from that union in case of a strike in order to bring it into line. Thirdly, "wage drift" (wages and earnings increases allowed by companies above the nationally-negotiated figures) during periods of restraint and the "wage explosions" (large and widely varying increases) that occurred in 1951 and 1955 after two years of wage restraint, indicate the pressures that build up among the rank-and-file and in the individual unions. In discussions with union officials and members in the Spring of 1956, the author found considerable sentiment in opposition to centrally-determined wage increases.

On non-wage matters, central negotiations, as already mentioned, are needed in order to expand the subjects covered by bargaining. With all negotiations concentrated in the early months of the year and with all settlements subject to SAF acceptance prior to employer association approval, the notion has prevailed that any non-wage advances would soon be generalized. Thus, a non-wage advance tends to be blocked until it is acceptable and applicable to all affiliates on both sides. That, of course, is a severe limitation on adaptation and innovation under national bargaining or even local bargaining, particularly as national bargains set the pattern for local negotiations.

Such restrictions on bargaining would be more significant if the Swedes were a tradition-bound people. They are, on the contrary, receptive to new ideas and modern methods, and pride themselves on being progressive. Swedish workers, for example, do not have the class restraints on the purchase of modern living conveniences that exist in Britain. Furthermore, the LO and the national unions use their extensive union education programs to convince officials and members of individual unions that it is desirable to accept new techniques and alterations in institutional relationships.

Although negotiations are calm and reasoned, national bargaining in Sweden is not confined to top levels, is not cut and dried, and has not developed a wide gap between high union officials and the rank-and-file. A wage conference composed of delegates from the union's locals both formulates the national's demands and selects a negotiating committee, of which a majority must be rank-and-filers. In the course of negotiations, the committee generally reports back to the conference at least once and, in some cases, a number of times. The duration and character of the negotiations varies from union to union and from year to year. In recent years, negotiations in most industries have consumed more time than formerly, and all-night sessions are not unusual. Generally speaking, Swedish negotiations are about as lengthy as they are in this country. A postwar change in LO statutes, however, weakens rank-and-file power to delay or reject proposed settlements by stipulating that the executive council of an affiliated union only has the power to make an agreement that binds the union. Ratification by the wage conference or the membership is not governing, and executive councils have accepted terms that were disapproved in a membership vote. Incidentally, the percentage of the membership voting on agreements or election of officers is generally higher in Sweden than in England. Voting statistics show that, on the average, one-third to two-fifths of all members vote on the question of extending an existing agreement or accepting a proposed new agreement.[10] The largest union, the Metal Workers with 235,000 members (out of a total of 1,400,000 in the forty-four national unions affiliated with LO) reports that total ballots on issues have recently been running between two-fifths and three-fifths of the eligible voters.[11]

Despite some centralization and expansion in union head-quarters' staffs, the top officials in the national unions seem to have been fairly successful in maintaining close contact with the locals and the membership. In spite of the size of the country, the top officers visit the locals frequently, which is facilitated by the size of unions there. Swedish unions hold many meetings and have extensive educational programs. Some observers believe that perhaps the most important achievement of the Swedish labor movement is the broadening of members' perspectives and the changing of their attitudes through discussion. Certainly good communication has reduced the likelihood of a significant gap or cleavage between the top officials and the general membership. Some who have studied both American and Swedish unionism believe that the channels of communication from the rank-and-file to the leadership are better in Sweden, which means more influence of the membership on the leadership than is generally true in this country.

Swedish unions do not appear to have experienced a decline in democratic checks and in vitality at the local level on the scale that has occurred in Great Britain. It is true that increasingly more decisions are being made at the national level and by full-time officials, and that the SAF strongly prefers greater union centralization, particularly more authority concentrated in LO. Also the national unions have a second-generation leadership and union presidents enjoy security of office, since they are always reelected without contest at conventions held every three to five years. However, Swedish unions have considerable participation by the rank-and-file in the determination of union policy, and the industrial-union setup in Sweden avoids the structural weaknesses, especially at the local level, prevalent in England. All Swedish unions have about the same pattern of government, educational activity, and membership participation. And, at the local level, they have real contests not only to win union office but also to be on a wage conference or to be a delegate to the union's convention. These contests are sharpened by a difference of views on union policy, especially where communists, representing about five per cent of the total union membership in Sweden, seek to gain influence and control.

A difference of opinion exists in Sweden as to whether the local unions have been losing some of their vitality and appeal during the past two decades. It is claimed that some reduction in the functions and effective decision-making at the local level has served to diminish attendance at meetings and the attraction of unionism for the younger generation. This question was discussed by the author with ten persons separately in Sweden who have a good basis for a judgment; they divided 50-50 in their opinions. It was also discussed with a group of fourteen members of twelve unions, two-thirds of whom thought that some decrease in vitality and interest had occurred in local unions during the past decade.

Those who doubted that any weakening of local unions had occurred pointed to the important functions left to be performed locally: (1) piece-rate negotiations, which influence the pay of two-thirds of all production hours; (2) works councils, dealing with production problems in the plant; (3) grievance handling; (4) union educational and recreational activities, which are primarily local; and (5) local political activities, which are tied in with the unions in many cases. They contended that in their unions attendance at local meetings was as high percentage-wise as formerly and explained that the number of grievances appealed to the national union-employers association level has recently been increasing in some unions. As further evidence of local vitality they cited the extent of "wage drift"—the rise in earnings relative to negotiated rates as a result of extra payments in one form or another including local pay increases and loose piece rates. In the period 1945 through 1956, wage drift is estimated to have amounted to three-quarters as much as the total negotiated increases.[12] Those who believe that some drying up at the local level has taken place supported their opinion with claims that in some unions: (1) attendance at local meetings had declined, (2) it was more difficult to interest members, and (3) the younger people were particularly inclined to be apathetic, partly perhaps because of full-employment in the postwar period. Under the circumstances, it is difficult to arrive at any positive conclusion, but perhaps a slight decline in vigor has developed in some unions.

Corruption has been no problem in unions in Sweden. The Swedish labor movement was early indoctrinated with the socialist tradition of working-class solidarity. The president of LO and the president of each affiliated union all receive the same salary, which is less than double the average earnings of members and is exceeded by the salaries of some staff experts of LO and national unions. The standards for salaries of labor officials are assumed to be different from those applied to union economists hired from outside the ranks of labor. Class sentiment is still strong in the Swedish labor movement, although it seems to be diminishing somewhat.

While Swedish unionism has matured in some respects, it still maintains some of the dynamic characteristics of a youthful movement. Partly this is because it bloomed relatively late and is not so hampered by long-standing traditions; partly it is because most union presidents are able men in their 40's subject to compulsory retirement at 60; partly it is because the rank-and-file participate in national bargaining; and partly it is because stress is placed on discussion and educational programs at all levels. Whatever the problem—whether handling grievances or dealing with wage increases—sufficient time and effort are devoted to make certain that it is an educational process on both sides.

Certain aspects of industrial relations in Sweden are typical of an advanced stage of development in union-management relations and in union policies. The "core of conflict" between the parties has narrowed considerably. Their relations are friendly, their negotiations are calm and reasoned, much joint machinery has been established, and the unions have adopted parts of personnel management and some of the responsibilities of management. The strike has been declining in significance, partly perhaps because of the existence of a Labor Government and more government intervention in negotiations, but also because the SAF has at times threatened an industry-wide or more general lock-out and the SAF is quite powerful in terms of control over its members and in financial resources. Increasing centralization within the labor movement and in collective bargaining is another attribute of maturity. In addition, the rate of innovation through collective bargaining has probably been declining, partly because national bargaining under the supervision of federations tends to restrict advances to the lowest common denominator. Interunion rivalry also seems to have declined somewhat, although there is some jockeying by national unions in wage negotiations and some competition is provided by the communists, the Syndicalists (with 20,000 members), and the white-collar and salaried-workers unions (42 organizations with 350,000 members, affiliated with a separate union federation).

Perhaps the most striking evidence that the Swedish labor movement has reached a fairly advanced stage of development is the broad, comprehensive view taken by union leaders and even many among the rank-and-file. They have come to accept responsibilities for the health of the nation's economy. Remarkable has been their willingness to adopt wage restraint so frequently as a means of combatting the inflationary dangers of a wage-price spiral. Indeed, a LO report as early as 1951 proposed that consideration be given to a less full-employment economy that would be subject to more fiscal manipulation in order that unions might avoid being forced into inflationary wage policies.[13]

Experience in Sweden seems to indicate that a labor movement can largely overcome the stagnating tendencies in the process of maturing, by such means as institutional arrangements for widespread participation in collective bargaining, reliance on democratic procedures and good internal communications, and a progressive spirit among the leadership and membership. The general environment and traditions also make some difference. As indicated in the next chapter, these same factors help to explain the diversity of experience in individual American unions.

VIII. EXPERIENCE IN INDIVIDUAL
UNIONS

THIS CHAPTER SURVEYS the evolutionary changes within five national unions. Those selected for brief examination are primarily the prominent ones that tend to dominate the labor movement. They are: the Amalgamated Clothing Workers, the United Automobile Workers, the Brotherhood of Carpenters, the Teamsters, and the United Mine Workers.

In reviewing the development of each of these organizations from the years of struggle and strife to the present, we shall be interested in the extent to which they have grown up and settled down. There is no presumption that the evolution of each conforms to a single, common pattern. Their backgrounds, experience, and leadership have been too diverse for that. We shall, however, be interested in the extent to which they have moved along in the same general directions, although often at different times and according to their own pace. The final section of the chapter will make cross-comparisons and examine the common elements in the evolution of the selected unions.

The Amalgamated Clothing Workers

In 1914, a rebel group of "progressives" seceded from the lethargic United Garment Workers Union and founded the Amalgamated Clothing Workers. The insurgents complained that the UGWU, a craft organization, was dominated by a political machine, composed of men who had grown old in office and who were out of touch with many of the rank-and-file factory workers.

Sidney Hillman was president of the new industrial union from its founding until his death in 1946. Thereafter the Amalgamated has been headed by a close associate from the early days, Jacob Potofsky. Indeed, almost all the present top leadership stems from the formative days before 1920 and prides itself in following the path of Hillman's leadership and policies. In the last membership referendum, all seventeen incumbent vice presidents on the Executive Board were reelected; in fact, over three-fourths of the union's Executive Board are the same persons who were on the Board a decade ago.

From the outset, the Amalgamated was considered one of the "most advanced" of American unions. During the first two decades of its existence, the union attempted a variety of pioneering ventures including the first full-fledged research department, an unemployment insurance plan, and cooperative banking, insurance, and housing programs. As the interests of the Amalgamated broadened into education, life insurance, medical care, and community affairs, there was talk of "the union as a way of life."

The Amalgamated began with a class-struggle orientation and with typically socialist aspirations. Many of its earlier organizers were ardent young socialists.[1] In the 1920's, the communists attempted unsuccessfully to capture the organization. Continued negotiations with the employers, however, led to more understandings and more collaboration. The union encouraged the formation of strong employer organizations, and since 1941 has dealt with the Clothing Manufacturers Association, which serves as the national employers' agency.

For over two decades industrial peace has prevailed; the Amalgamated has had no national or notable strikes. New agreements are negotiated with little commotion. During years of slack demand for clothing, such as the three years

[90]

from 1947 to 1950, the union has not pressed for wage increases. Partly because of economic conditions in the industry, the union no longer is a pacemaker and pioneer in collective bargaining. The Amalgamated has cooperated with manufacturers to improve efficiency and production in the shop. Indeed, in a number of respects, including recruitment and training, the union has served as an industrial relations department for the industry. So much good will and respect exist in the industry that a number of men's clothing manufacturers testified against provisions in the bill that later became the Taft-Hartley Act, and, right after the Act's passage, the industry signed five-year union-shop agreements in order to help the union evade the law's union-security restrictions.

Although the joint board composed of local unions in a city is a strong union center, the strength and power of the national headquarters has increased since national bargaining, covering 95 per cent of the industry, commenced in 1937. In 1939, the Amalgamated began a wage stabilization program, which is supervised by a headquarters' Wage Stabilization Department, to assure that labor costs for the same grade of garment are roughly equivalent in each production center. Furthermore, in order to limit competition and prevent wage-cutting, the union has reorganized the industry's structure, eliminating competitive bidding among contractors and increasing the responsibility of the jobber and manufacturer.

In many respects, the Amalgamated has exhibited a typical metamorphosis. It has developed from insurgency to integration, from militancy to collaboration, from pioneering to the extension of existing programs. In a sense, the Amalgamated reflects the life development of one man—Sidney Hillman—and it is as though his life, instead of ending in mid-1946 at age 60, were still continuing and providing the cooperative leadership and settled outlook of his union.[2]

The United Automobile Workers

In many respects the United Automobile, Aircraft and Agricultural Implement Workers of America is an unusual union. Built from the bottom up, it has continued to maintain considerable vigor, missionary zeal, and pioneering qualities, despite the elimination of the turbulence and factionalism that characterized the first dozen years of UAW's existence (1935-1947). The dynamic quality of this union stems partly from its early struggles and partly from the idealism and progressive character of its leadership.

Until 1947, the UAW had a stormy history. It was torn by inner conflict and stirred by violent employer opposition. Various factions—socialists, Lovestonites, followers of the Communist Party line, progressives, and what not—vied for power until Walter Reuther gained control of the national organization in the 1947 convention. The first president, Homer Martin, was forced out after three years in office. The second president, R. J. Thomas, held on for seven years amid continued jockeying between the Reuther faction and that spearheaded by Secretary-Treasurer George Addes, who tended to follow the Communist Party line. At a number of critical points, the rank-and-file rose and took decisive action without direction from the top officials. That was the case, for instance, in the sit-down strikes of 1936 and 1937, and again in the Ford walkout in 1941. Out of such experience there developed a tradition of democracy and an active political life within the organization.

Most of the top leadership of the UAW participated in the early struggles to organize the union, and some of them were members of the Socialist Party in the 1930's. The chief officers average perhaps 50 years of age; they were strongly influenced by the Great Depression and the New Deal. Much the same is true of the regional directors and headquarters staff of the UAW. They have a youthful quality and generally are progressive in outlook. The union's philosophy is evident in its newspaper and monthly magazine, which frequently are critical of management views and programs. Like President Reuther, most of the UAW hierarchy consider their union to be an extraordinary, pioneering institution, destined to make a difference in the social and political climate in this country.

Since 1947, Reuther has consolidated his power and has developed a smooth-running organization. At the national level, solidarity has replaced schism, and continuous leadership for a decade has given the union stability. A highly capable staff has been recruited from within and from outside, particularly from the government and other unions. Indeed, four well-trained unionists were recruited externally for UAW staff jobs in 1957. The result is that the Auto Workers have the largest and most capable staff of any American union.

Opposition to the Reuther leadership has steadily dwindled since 1947 and now is chiefly to be found in a few locals, including the big Ford Local 600 at River Rouge. Within the union, criticism is not so much in terms of bargaining goals as of Reuther personally and his methods. Indeed, in the 1957 convention, the Executive Board's recommendations on crucial issues, such as separate ratification of agreements by skilled workers and a dues increase, were accepted by overwhelming majorities; so strong was the position of the national leadership that for the first time since Reuther became president there was insufficient opposition to obtain a single roll-call vote at a UAW convention. So much unity now exists in the organization that some auto executives profess to be disturbed by the lack of diversity of ideas within the UAW.[3]

Evidently Walter Reuther has achieved a position in the Auto Workers roughly equivalent to that which Sidney Hillman enjoyed in the Amalgamated. Reuther's dedication to the cause, his broad vision, and his bold and imaginative proposals have tended to set the tone for the union, but it is far from a one-man show. Reuther is surrounded by a group of highly capable lieutenants, and the tradition of rank-and-file independence exists although its exercise has diminished. The situation of the UAW in the auto industry is one without a parallel. Consequently, one cannot simply assume that the Auto Workers now are at the stage, say, which the Amalgamated reached in the 1920's.

Despite long-term agreements running three and five years and despite the absence of a significant company-wide strike in autos since 1950, the UAW seems to have lost relatively little of its drive. Management decisions and technological changes continue to create employee complaints and grievances. Indeed, in General Motors the number of grievances per 1,000 workers has increased since 1953. In negotiations, the union has skillfully played one of the large auto firms against the other two and has used single-plant strikes over production standards, which are permitted, as a means of making long-term contracts into "living documents."

Some writers think that a transformation has already commenced in the internal life and character of the UAW. As evidence, they point to the lack of opposition to the leadership, to centralizing tendencies, to increasing bureaucracy and reliance on experts, and to the lack of new organizational gains in recent years.[4] The very size of the organization, with some one and a third million members, contributes to an enlargement of the distance from the bottom to the top of the union pyramid.

Despite such developments, the UAW so far seems to have lost little of its momentum. It is still pioneering, seeking to spread the scope of bargaining further and to extend the union's political activities. Whether its innovating possibilities have been reduced is difficult to determine, because of the imaginative, progressive leadership at the top. It will be interesting to see whether the union's democratic traditions, its educational program, and the capable group surrounding Reuther will be able to prevent any tendency for the UAW to settle down to a more normal union existence.[5]

The Carpenters

For two decades after its founding in 1881, the United Brotherhood of Carpenters and Joiners of America was characterized by an evangelical, pioneering brand of trade unionism under President Peter J. McGuire, a dedicated socialist.[6] It was at the forefront of the movement for the eight-hour day in the 1880's. The union then was a loose organization—decentralized, democratic, and subject to internal struggles for control.

After the turn of the century, however, political machines developed both nationally and locally under the business agents. The power of the national union increased, largely in order to protect and expand the jurisdiction of the Carpenters in the face of threats from other building trades. Jurisdictional issues and alliances could be well handled only on a national scale.

By 1917, a system of centralized control and political unity had been firmly established under President William L. Hutcheson. Since 1912, the president has been the chairman of the union's executive board, each of whose members is in charge of a region, whereas he has overall responsibility. He can issue and revoke charters, suspend locals and district councils of the union, suspend union officers, and make and break local agreements. The organizers are appointed by and under the direction of the president, who also appoints the members of the committees for the five-year conventions of the union.

For the past four decades, the Carpenters have been dominated by the conservative leadership of William Hutcheson (president from 1915 to 1952) and of his son Maurice (president since 1952), both Republicans and Masons of high standing. A communist opposition and noncommunist dissent were crushed in the early 1920's and no real opposition to the top leadership has existed in the Carpenters since then. No contest for the union's presidency has occurred since 1924. On some occasions, the elder Hutcheson aroused the ire of locals by peremptorily siding with employers against particular locals, but in recent years the union has operated smoothly.

The Carpenters have generally been on good terms with the employers with whom they deal. Usually negotiations are conducted with an employers' association on an area basis. The local business agents, having power to dispense jobs and to call strikes, serve as sort of labor contractors. Their strong positions have made them relatively conservative and have contributed to corruption and racketeering in the union.

The amount of national control is somewhat surprising in a union having a membership of 835,000 in 3,000 locals and operating in an industry with a localized market and with collective bargaining principally on a local or area basis. Power has been concentrated in the national office mainly on jurisdictional grounds, although the large funds for retirement, disability, and death benefits have also aided somewhat in the location of power in the headquarters.

During the past thirty years the United Brotherhood has been a staid, businesslike union. Some locals and district councils have vitality and exercise considerable power, but the union generally has shown the signs of maturity for some time. Its reformist, crusading days were ended by World War I; even its membership has grown relatively old.

The Teamsters

Since its founding in 1902, the International Brotherhood of Teamsters, Chauffeurs, Warehousemen and Helpers of America has grown to a union with almost a million and a half members. For the first forty-five years the Teamsters was a decentralized union with a high degree of local autonomy. During the post-World War II period, however, influence and power have been gradually shifting to the regional level, under an evident trend toward centralization.[7]

The economic strength of the Teamsters rests on its control over truck transportation. As long as horse-drawn and truck transportation remained local-market industries, the joint council of locals in a city, often dominated by one or two leaders, were the center of gravity and control in the union. The business agent, who frequently negotiated contracts and settled grievances himself, was an important figure. However, as the employing firms expanded geographically and over-the-road trucking assumed increasing significance, the need for regional uniformity and a single negotiation for a nation-wide firm became more evident. Much of the industry, of course, still retains its local-market character but expansion in intercity and regional trucking has tended to develop greater power in the regional and national offices of the union. In the face of these economic changes and pressures, the leaders of the local joint councils have, of course, vigorously sought to maintain their authority and autonomy, and they have been partially successful, particularly in large cities like New York and Chicago. A tradition of local autonomy, built up over decades, has not been easily altered; centralization has been resisted by members of the union's general executive board because they might thereby lose some of the power they exercise locally.

The first decade and a half of the union's existence were characterized by internecine strife and secession movements. Thereafter, the Brotherhood settled down to a decentralized existence, with the national union serving as a sort of federation of the strong local units. From 1907 until his retirement in 1952, Daniel J. Tobin was unanimously reelected as president. However, he could not control the union's conventions nor was he able to extend the power of the national union over the locals to any significant extent. Repeatedly the conventions rejected Tobin's pet scheme to establish a national death benefit program, which would have increased the national union's influence by giving it a fund in which individual members had an equity. The executive board also denied Dave Beck, Tobin's successor, any authority to control the pension and welfare funds of local, state, and regional units.

Beck developed a strong position in the union through the Western Conference of Teamsters, which he established in 1937, with representatives of the joint councils and locals in the eleven Western states. Under the Conference he also established trade divisions for the region on the basis of type of work—bakery drivers, beverage, dairy, over-the-road, and so forth. Beck thus gained considerable control over the affairs of the Brotherhood in the entire region for a period of ten years before the formation of conferences was recognized constitutionally. After the formation of three more conferences—Southern (in 1943) and Central and Eastern (in 1953)—agreements began to be negotiated on a regional basis in order to obtain uniformity on an interstate level. Such area-wide arrangements have been strongly pressed by James Hoffa, head of the Conference of the twelve Central states, who has successfully persuaded local unions to relinquish their autonomy in order to achieve state and regional uniformity.

After Dave Beck became president in 1952, he sought to centralize more power in the national office but without too much success. Supervisory control over welfare and trust funds was denied the president and, although he established national trade divisions, so far they have exerted little real influence. The president has the power to appoint the organizers, the chairmen of the conferences, and trustees to take charge of the affairs of errant local unions, which can be an extremely effective device for controlling locals. About 12 per cent of the Brotherhood's locals were under such trusteeships in 1957, and over one-quarter of those trusteeships had continued for more than five years.[8] The president also determines whether strike benefits will be paid from the national's funds—the Western Conference has its own special fund for strike benefits to supplement those that the national pays.

The Teamsters' leaders, particularly Beck and Hoffa, have been among the leading exponents of strictly "business unionism." They have visualized themselves as sort of glorified labor contractors on large salaries and enjoying a good standard of living, including Cadillac cars, to which the representatives of Hoffa's Detroit local are entitled for the performance of their union duties.[9]

As mentioned in Chapter VI, the Senate Select Committee received more complaints about racketeering and undemocratic practices from members of the Teamsters than from any other union. The Committee's hearings also exposed the extensive business connections of Teamsters' leaders and their ties with the underworld. So long as the leadership can negotiate good contracts, however, the rank-and-file seem rather unconcerned with loss of local autonomy or even graft by individual leaders. The influence of the AFL-CIO was insufficient to prevent Hoffa from being elected president in the 1957 Convention despite threats to expel the Teamsters if they failed to conform to the Federation's code of ethics.

The Mine Workers

During the past three decades, the United Mine Workers of America, with over half a million members, has been one of the most centralized unions in this country. Control has been concentrated in the hands of John L. Lewis, who has been president of the union since 1920.

Prior to the Lewis regime, the Mine Workers was a highly

democratic union with a robust political life.[10] It was almost a federation of autonomous districts, which were principally state-wide. The district presidents exercised considerable power, and strongly favored decentralized procedures. In the 1920's, Lewis changed all that, largely by suspending and expelling officials and locals that dared to challenge his leadership. By building up a machine of loyal lieutenants, he obtained complete and unquestioned authority over the whole organization.

The economics of the industry also has contributed to centralization of the Mine Workers. In order to achieve unity of action in both bargaining and striking in an industry spread over 5,000 employers in twenty-seven states, some central control of policy and strategy was necessary. The bulk of the market for the product is national, substitute fuels have been a growing threat, and the problems of non-union competition and unauthorized strikes have at times been troublesome for the union. To meet such conditions and problems required national policies and actions. The system of regional bargaining under the Central Competitive Field Agreements broke down in the 1920's and was replaced by national bargaining in the 1930's. The consequence of such developments has been that the function of collective bargaining, including the formulation of demands, has been lost at the local level; the locals and district organizations have become largely administrative agencies for the national union.

The union's constitution has also facilitated centralized control by one man. Under the constitution, the president can appoint all organizers, staff, and convention committees and "may suspend or remove any International Officer [including Executive Board members] or appointed employee for insubordination or just and sufficient cause" subject to the approval of the Executive Board, a majority of which has consisted of Lewis' appointees. He may revoke the charters of locals and subdistrict and district units and has the authority to "create a provisional government" in units where a charter has been revoked. Under those powers, districts representing a half to three-quarters of the voting power in the union have operated under "provisional" control of the president for more than two decades. In addition to those powers for discouraging potential opposition, the constitution provides that "It shall be illegal to contribute funds for the promotion of the candidacy of any candidate for office within the Organization" and that "Any member guilty of slandering or circulating, or causing to be circulated, false statements about any member or any members, circulating or causing to be circulated any statement wrongfully condemning any decision rendered by an officer of the Organization, shall, upon conviction, be suspended from membership for a period of six months and shall not be eligible to hold office in any branch of the Organization for two years thereafter."

Democracy has not been snuffed out in large sections of the union without an occasional request from a convention delegate for election rather than appointment of managers of district offices. President Lewis' reply takes the form of posing as alternatives either an "efficient organization" or a "political instrumentality," either "the most efficient instrumentality within the realm of possibility for a labor organization" or the sacrifice of efficiency for "a little more academic freedom in the selection of some" representatives.[11]

So successful has Lewis been in achieving economic gains for the membership in the form of wages and benefits that a study in the early 1950's of rank-and-file sentiment in a district under Lewis appointees for over twenty years revealed little criticism of one-man rule and the suppression of democratic rights. The study concluded from interviews with workers in various industries that acquiescence to authoritarian control and diminished membership participation in union activities had "perhaps" developed further in the Mine Workers than in any of the other unions whose members were interviewed.[12] There is little evidence that the members begrudge President Lewis his $50,000 salary or the Vice-President and the Secretary-Treasurer their salaries of $40,000 each.

Not only has the organization been subject to one-man control; the same has been true of negotiations for new contract terms. As mentioned in Chapters III and VI, bargaining in bituminous coal since 1950 has been carried on in secret between one man from each side—for the union by Lewis and, in 1956, by Vice-President Kennedy. The membership generally becomes aware of negotiations after a settlement (deal?) has been made. In the 1956 convention a few delegates suggested (complained is too strong a word) that the new agreement might have included provision for shorter hours in order to relieve some local pockets of unemployed miners, but the agreement was accepted without a dissenting vote.[13]

Since 1950 no major strike has occurred in the soft coal industry, and the national union has been bearing down on any unauthorized strikes with fines and threat of expulsion of individual members.[14] In contrast, during the thirteen years ending with 1950 national stoppages took place, on the average, every eighteen months. The change from grass-roots militancy to mutual accommodation under the new technique of two-man "rational" bargaining was praised by President Lewis in telling the 1956 convention:

"It augurs well for the future. For six years now there have been no major stoppages in the industry, and for an indefinite period into the future that will continue, providing the leaders of the industry on both sides continue to exercise that discretion and judgment which they have now exhibited that they possess."[15]

That the Mine Workers as an organization has settled down to a rather calm and peaceful existence is abundantly evident. In the 1920's, the 1930's, or the 1940's, few would have predicted that the characteristics of union maturity would be so evident in this union by the mid-1950's.

Similarity of Development

In selecting five unions for individual examination, an effort was made to discuss the more prominent ones and a diversified group in terms of background and experience. In the selection, building construction, transportation, and mining are represented as well as manufacturing. All five developed from the bottom up and not from the top down as in the case of the Steelworkers. The five together represent almost five million members.

Despite apparent diversity, many threads of common development are evident. Generally speaking, the older the union, the sooner signs of maturity begin to appear. Of course, such a conclusion needs to be modified by the nature of the industry and peculiarities of institutional development. The auto industry, with vigorous intercompany rivalry and rapid technological change, helps to create a different employee and union psychology from that in a contracting industry like coal or an undynamic industry like men's clothing. The newest union, the Automobile Workers, does seem to be more youthful, pioneering, and internally vigorous than any of the others. Nevertheless even that union shows some evidence of a shift of influence toward the national headquarters, a disappearance of significant opposition within the organization, and a willingness by the rank-and-file to let the leadership determine policy and run the union.

In the other four unions, the trend toward maturity is pronounced. The elements in that trend include: increasing centralization and machine control, a shift from class-struggle radicalism to moderation and accommodation with management, a decline in the rate of membership expansion and

[103]

in pioneering and missionary zeal, and a significant decrease in the use of the strike weapon.

The rapidity and character of these trends varies, of course, in the individual unions. And if one could, so to speak, abstract these trend developments, marked contrasts would remain. For instance, the scope of the Amalgamated's activities is much broader than that of the Carpenters, the Teamsters, or the Mine Workers. Significant differences also exist in such matters as the vigor of internal union life, the effectiveness of democratic checks, and the role of corrupt influences.

Nevertheless the evidence of a common drift or common trends, despite considerable diversity of inheritance and environment, is noteworthy. It is too marked and general to be dismissed as random variation or to be ascribed to personal characteristics of a particular union leadership. Doubtless it reflects in considerable measure, the operation of underlying forces and impersonal compulsions.

IX. THE THEORY OF UNION
DEVELOPMENT

THE CHANGING CHARACTER of American unions and the factors underlying the changes were discussed in Chapters III, IV, V, and VI. The evolution of English and Swedish unionism was analyzed in Chapter VII, and Chapter VIII examined the factors that help to explain developments of particular American unions. On the basis of that material, this chapter seeks to construct the framework for a general theory of union development and to indicate the applicability of such a theory.

As already explained, there is no uniform pattern of evolution that all unions must travel so that one can observe a union and place it in stage 1, 2, 3, or 4. Union development is too varied and dissimilar to be categorized into sharply defined stages. Consequently, the theoretical structure presented here will be in terms of (1) general tendencies and long-run trends and (2) dynamic or cyclical variation from such trends. Treatment of general tendencies will be divided into (a) processes of internal union development and (b) processes of external integration, somewhat along the lines of Chapters III and IV. The discussion of dynamic upswings and plateaus will be in terms of reinvigorating factors—breakthroughs into new areas, external and internal disturbances, competition, etc.—and the settling-down process following an upswing. As explained in Chapter V, the decelerating influences grow out of declining opportunities for union exploitation and internal changes that accompany the ageing of successful labor institutions. The final section of

[105]

the chapter will discuss the limitations of the analytical structure constructed from these elements.

General Tendencies and Long-run Trends

The stress in this book has been on underlying forces and processes in institutional development. That is not intended to belittle the importance of the coloration that an institution acquires in its early years. The formative cast is not easily altered, as the UAW and Swedish unionism clearly illustrate. Nor for a representative agency such as a union should one underrate the significance of the element of security— security for the institution and security for the present leadership. Union maturity rests heavily on both types of security. Security, stability, and preoccupation with administration are moderating influences in social institutions.

As unions age, they are prone to experience internal adjustments similar to those that take place in other institutions which in their formative years had to struggle for existence and acceptance. In the case of labor unions the gradual alterations that occur through the processes of internal change can be classified under three headings: (1) a decline in the rate of expansion and missionary zeal, (2) a shift of power and control toward the national headquarters, and (3) an alteration in the union's leadership.

Each of these developments was discussed in Chapter III. As a union's growth curve begins to level off, subtle psychological changes tend to take place. The turbulence and enthusiasm of youth, the missionary zeal of a new movement, slow down to a more moderate pace. Increasingly, decisions are made centrally, as a political machine becomes entrenched, as the channels of union communication are more tightly controlled from the top, and as reliance on staff specialists expands. Along with these changes, the national leadership experiences some modification. As the organization enlarges, the problems of management multiply and the emphasis shifts from organization to administration, negotiation, and contract enforcement. The leaders of the formative years are succeeded by a second and a third generation leadership, who did not experience the early struggles and bitterness. Security for the top hierarchy and the good life on a sizeable salary, as explained in Chapter VI, may be part of a group of corrupting influences. The democratic checks may have weakened with increasing size, centralization, and power in the hands of full-time functionaries. Such developments are natural in the evolution of successful institutions serving as representatives of interest groups.

Interest-group representation aimed at altering the distribution of rights and privileges also undergoes a process of external integration. Societal acceptance and partial absorption tend to accompany success in achieving some of the organization's goals. As explained in Chapter IV, with institutional security and additional bargaining experience, the amount of joint machinery increases, the union acquires respectability, and its interests broaden. The success that the union has in satisfying workers' non-wage desires tends to diversify and diffuse its goals. It moves into community welfare activities, into public education, and even into farm programs. In other words, its focus widens, and its activities become generalized. All this is part of the settling-in process.

To summarize, the processes of internal change develop long-run trends toward internal stability, centralization, and machine control; the processes of external integration encourage a long-range tendency toward accommodation, orderly and peaceful arrangements, and breadth and moderation. Although the direction of the drift is unmistakable, the pace of movement may vary considerably so that, in the case of certain unions, two or three decades may be necessary for some of these long-run trends to begin to be evident.

Short-term Swings

The trends are often obscured by periods of revival, arising out of economic or political disturbances, threats to the union or its leadership, or union advances into new areas. These swings or tides in union affairs do not have a regular periodicity nor are they necessarily all-pervasive. Some disturbances and adjustments are confined to particular industries or sections of the country; while one union is experiencing rapid innovation, another may be languishing in semi-stagnation. Consequently, organized labor as a whole may present a variegated picture. The union movement lacks the general, constant pressure on all industry that is generated by competition for the consumer's dollar, nor does it have the political party's all embracing stimulus of a national election every four years. Worker discontent is less general because it is plant-oriented, and periodic negotiations by autonomous unions are scattered and sporadic in contrast with a nationwide election campaign.

Nevertheless the labor movement does experience periods of extensive ferment and fairly general advance followed by consolidation and levelling-off to a plateau. Ferment is generated by disturbances and strains that require readjustments and stimulate worker protest; general advance hinges to a considerable extent on favorable economic and political conditions. Usually unions have experienced upswings in membership during wars and inflations and loss of momentum during postwar eras.

Cyclical-like shifts in public sentiment affect the climate that surrounds union activities. That sentiment is reflected not only in political developments and employer attitudes toward unions but also in the general cultural atmosphere. The New Deal of the 1930's was followed, after the war, by the Eisenhower era of moderation. The dozen years after World War II saw no increase, and perhaps even a slight decline, in the percentage of the organizable labor force who were union members,[1] and, although there were no organized employer campaigns against unions such as those following World War I, various types of restrictive labor legislation were enacted by Congress and the state legislatures.

Occasionally, forces within the labor movement may play an important role in general union reinvigoration, as experience in the 1930's demonstrated. The competition and rivalry of the newly-formed CIO stimulated the AFL unions. Such challenges provoke unions to organize and be enterprising. As noted in Chapter v, some degree of employer hostility and even adverse legislation, if not too destructive, may prove wholesome to an opposition-type institution which is prone to languish in the midst of industrial peace. Bargaining breakthroughs and organizational expansion not only upset a stable situation and generate union imitation and competition, but also they stimulate employer opposition. The resulting friction is usually reflected in strike statistics, which normally rise with the spread of unionism, with union efforts to pioneer, and with an increase in union rivalry.[2]

In contrast, strike statistics contract during stable periods. The amount of challenge is reduced when intra-union and interunion rivalry decline under emphasis on labor unity and when a shrinkage occurs both in the area of conflict between the parties and in the opportunities for unions to exploit. Such shrinkage grows out of settlement of some of the big issues dividing the parties in the early years and elimination of differences between blue- and white-collar workers, with rising living standards and greater equalization of non-wage terms and conditions of employment. Also, as negotiating experience accumulates, union leaders tend to develop good personal relations with employers and to acquire an understanding and sympathy for the problems of business management. A metamorphosis in the viewpoint of top union leaders may arise partly because their lives come closer to those of management. Under those conditions, unions may take on more and more of the attributes of "sleepy monopolies." The top leadership is less impelled or inclined to strive to achieve maximum possible gain for the membership, and the union itself may be more subject to use of its power and resources for financial advantage of the officialdom.

The process of settling down after an upswing is reinforced by underlying trends. Indeed, the slow-down and stability following an upswing largely represent the long-run tendencies reassuming a predominant role, and the downswing and the long-run trends tend to merge, for they are influenced primarily by the same factors and forces. Some of those influences are mentioned in the preceding paragraph, and earlier chapters have explained more fully the significant factors behind long-run trends.

Should the long-run drift toward a more orderly and structured existence for unions continue as it has during the past decade, one could expect dynamic upswings to become weaker, shorter, and less frequent. The factors discussed in this and preceding chapters point, on balance, to more years of stability and comparative tranquility in the future and hence relatively fewer years of resurgence, disturbance, and conquest for organized labor in America. Of course external events (such as inflations, wars, and even technological advance like rapid automation) or a big breakthrough (such as rapid organization of the South or of white-collar workers) might cause a sufficiently strong and sustained upswing so that the direction of the general drift might even seem to have been reversed. However, the balance of fundamental forces is such that a permanent alteration of direction in long-run trends seems exceedingly doubtful—at least in the foreseeable future.

Summary of the Theory

The subject matter under investigation does not lend itself to simple, rigorous theorizing. The diversity of experience, features, and programs of American unions makes generalization hazardous and a systematic body of abstract theory practically impossible. That is especially the case where the objective is to explain the pattern of development of institutions over a period of time.

Nevertheless a structure of analysis and a set of conclusions concerning trends have been presented, and it may be helpful to summarize that analytical framework and the main conclusions in outline form.

A. General tendencies and long-run trends grow out of
   1. the processes of internal union development and
   2. the processes of external integration.
B. Short-term swings around long-run trends develop from
   1. dynamic disturbances and strains (such as organizational expansion, increased competition, and technological change) and
   2. stability-restoring influences, which include factors contributing to long-run trends.

The conclusions with respect to general tendencies and long-run trends in American unionism are as follows:

1. As the rate of union expansion slows down, a psychological ageing tends to spread throughout the organization, especially if it already covers most of its jurisdiction.

2. With the passage of time and the accumulation of experience, central control at union headquarters tends to expand and democratic checks at the local level weaken.

3. As a union stabilizes and ages, the top leadership becomes more administrative in character and the differences between union executives and management executives diminish.

[111]

4. The more successes unions achieve, the more they tend to reduce their areas of potential expansion and innovation and, consequently, some of their dynamic qualities.

5. With increased bargaining experience and rising living standards, the differences between manual and white-collar workers tend to narrow and the areas of conflict and worker protest tend to be reduced.

6. As unions gain employer acceptance and their objectives broaden, the differences between unions and other community organizations tend to decrease.

7. Increasing security for the union and for the present leadership serves as a moderating influence; less rivalry and fewer challenges reduce the pressures and incentives for militant exploitation of a union's bargaining power.

It is predicted that these long-run tendencies and trends will continue in effectiveness over the forthcoming decades, tending to level out in some cases but not being completely offset or reversed.

Conclusions with respect to short-term movements or swings are as follows:

1. Such movements cause actual developments to deviate from the long-run trends but generally do not basically alter the latter, and the influence of the trends predominates over long periods of time.

2. Dynamic upswings that affect much of the labor movement may be promoted by a variety of external developments or even by a general internal upheaval like the founding of the CIO in the mid-1930's.

3. Years of disturbance, strain, and challenge for trade unionism are followed by periods of deceleration and comparative stability, when the short-run factors and long-run trends tend to merge, with the long-term tendencies predominating.

4. Assuming that the general tendencies and long-run

trends noted above continue to operate far into the future, the upswings should prove to be progressively less significant from decade to decade; this prediction rests on the hypothesis that long-run factors will increasingly predominate as time passes and experience accumulates.

Limitations and Qualifications

Obviously, these conclusions are tentative, subject to further substantiation or modification. For the most part they constitute informed but inadequately-verified hypotheses, which need to be subjected to extensive testing. Such testing could include independent analyses of experience during the past two decades and also during earlier periods. Future development over a decade or more will likewise provide a test of the validity of these hypotheses.

Similarly, the theoretical framework of long-run trends and short-term swings needs to be applied more extensively and to be elaborated in the light of critical examination by others. At this stage, the only claim that can be made is that it seems to provide a handy tool for analyzing the broad developments in American trade unionism during recent decades.

One limitation of the body of theory here expounded is its long-run character. It is not intended to provide an adequate explanation of short-term shifts and certainly not to predict the developments in a particular union. The analysis is at too high a level of generality or abstraction for that sort of detailed application. Moreover, as the discussion in Chapter VIII indicated, an individual union like the UAW may prevent, at least for a period, most long-run forces from having significant effects upon that organization.

Even in terms of its long-run perspective, some union and management officials may object to the analysis and for much the same reasons. Out of their personal experience they may doubt that the dynamic qualities of unions tend to diminish; in their view the thrust of unionism to expand and make new conquests continues and seems likely to remain unabated. Many managements still fear invasion of their prerogatives, and many labor leaders point to the variety of anti-union activities still present in different sectors of the economy. At the same time, persons loyal to the union ideal may question whether fundamental changes have occurred within the American labor movement as a whole. They may point to the operation of various countervailing factors, may stress the importance of the activities still performed by local unions, and claim that emphasis on selected trends leads to a warped appraisal.[3]

Speculation about the evolutionary process in trade unionism is at such an early stage that divergent types of analysis and interpretation should be welcomed. The theoretical structure and conclusions developed here represent one approach and one theoretical construct. Whether they constitute the most fruitful attack on the problem can only be determined from additional investigation and experience.

X. THE EVOLUTION OF
UNION-MANAGEMENT RELATIONS

THE SIGNIFICANCE of management policies for union development has already been considered in Chapter IV. Changes in the philosophy of business management during the past three decades were discussed, with particular reference to the shift from a commodity concept to respectful treatment of individual employees. The accommodation of managements to unions as experience with collective bargaining accumulates was also briefly examined.

The focus of this chapter is on trends in union-management relations, particularly viewed in the light of the conclusions of the preceding chapter. First, there will be a discussion of long-run tendencies and trends in management similar to those in unions and the interactions of such common developments. Second, trends in collective bargaining will be analyzed, drawing on material in previous chapters. Finally, some predictions will be hazarded concerning the direction of future developments in collective bargaining.

The discussion will be chiefly in terms of large corporations and industrial unions. They represent the dominant element in industrial relations in this country, tending to set the tone and patterns for medium-sized and small firms to follow.

Common Trends

Several of the tendencies operating within unions have had their counterparts in the large corporation. Undoubtedly, certain developments in both stem from the same causes.

Also, between changes in unions and changes in management considerable reaction and interaction have occurred. For instance, centralization in the industrial relations policies of management generates a corresponding tendency within the unions dealing with that management, and, similarly, management tends to react in the same direction to union centralizing developments.

Often it is in the top echelons of management and unions that most convergent development occurs. At the top, interests and viewpoints on both sides frequently are close. Both are administering large organizations and, as already explained, not only do they face some of the same problems but also the way of life of high management and top union officials is becoming less dissimilar.

Both corporations and unions have been experiencing a broadening of interest. Much stress has been placed on the increasing social conscience and public spirit of American management as its interests have extended into such areas as agricultural policy and foreign aid as well as the community chest and college education.[1] A corresponding development in unions was discussed in Chapter IV.

The professionalization of top officials and greater reliance on experts is a second common development. During the postwar period, American management has emphasized executive training and development, including courses and tests of various types. In addition, the number of persons in industrial relations activities in companies has expanded significantly since the 1920's. A 1957 study covering 714 concerns spread throughout the country showed that, on the average, they had one person engaged in personnel activities for every 125 employees.[2] That compares with an estimate of one full-time union official for every 300 members in American unions.[3] On the union side, the only program of executive training, which comes near to the company recruitment and training activities, is the one-year program conducted by the International Ladies' Garment Workers' Union for a group, the majority of whom has had some college experience. Nevertheless, as in the case of management, unions are making more and more use of staff experts —economists, lawyers, educators, journalists, and public-relations specialists. And union officials often employ them much as business executives do.

Another trend in the management of both companies and unions has been emphasis on and reward for "the organization man"—the person who accepts the values of the in-group and conforms to the thinking and program of the top management. William H. Whyte, Jr. has drawn an arresting picture of this pattern of group-thinking and "belongingness" in corporations.[4] A corresponding picture, differing somewhat in detail, could be painted of the subtle and not so subtle pressures to conform within the union hierarchy. Selection, training, and pruning to a particular image are developments likely to be characteristic of maturity, when a settled pattern has emerged.

The forces causing increasing centralization of functions and authority in many unions were discussed in Chapter iii. A similar development has taken place in the industrial relations activities of corporations. A comparative study of 13 large firms for the years 1938, 1947, and 1953 showed a continuing trend toward the centralization of their industrial relations. Despite considerable management opinion favoring decentralization, actual developments in labor policy were in the opposite direction—toward more functions handled by company headquarters in multiplant firms and at a high level in the management hierarchy.[5] Faced with strong unions, top business management has felt a need for close control of labor relations in order to gain and enforce uniformity in policies. The result is that industrial relations policies now, with few exceptions, are determined at the headquarters, and implementing procedures are largely formulated at that level too. The extensive study in 1953, covering 135 companies with three and a half million employees, found no evidence that the trend toward having top management exercise responsibility for important company decisions in industrial relations was likely to be reversed in the future.[6]

Management centralization of decisions on labor matters has affected union opinion and practice. That is indicated by a companion study of union decision-making levels, based on interviews with 28 staff and elected officials in 13 national unions with over five million members in 1953.[7] The unionists likewise favored centralization of policy-determination and, to some extent, policy implementation, even though they recognized the likelihood of devitalizing effects at the local level. As in the case of corporate management, headquarters decision-making was favored in order to achieve uniformity of policy and of its application. In addition, union officials stressed administrative efficiency and the need for use of trained experts for such matters as pensions, supplementary unemployment benefits, and the techniques of scientific management. Moreover, national legislation increasing potential union liabilities, particularly the Taft-Hartley Act, has promoted reliance upon experts on the staff of the national union. To some extent each side has sought to equal or exceed the other in expertness and sophistication in industrial relations. Such competition has tended to push up the level of decision-making within both organizations.

Of course, not all large corporations or unions have been subject to these common developments. Nevertheless, a general pattern of thinking, spread by contagion and imitation, is characteristic of American management in large concerns. For a variety of reasons, one of which is security, their leadership tends to conform to the main drift. Professional management, in contrast to one-man control, usually is sufficiently flexible to adjust its thinking and policies over a period of time. After all, one of its principal functions is to develop workable compromises.

All this is not to overlook basic distinctions between corporations and unions, such as differences with respect to competition and democratic checks or with respect to the operation of research and innovation. Nor is it to ignore deviations such as the stiffer attitude toward unions recently taken by a few large firms, of which the General Electric Company's program of contesting the union leadership's representation has been a notable example.[8] However, these tangential moves have not attracted sufficient followers to reverse any trends, nor is it likely in the future that hardboiled programs to short-circuit and challenge the basis of unions will gain much greater adherence among large firms.[9]

Trends in Collective Bargaining

Collective bargaining is a dynamic and often a cumulative process. As explained in Chapter IV, bargaining experience frequently serves as instructor and stabilizer. The parties come to know and understand one another. Management becomes more aware of the kind of organization a union is and especially of the internal workings of the particular unions with which it deals. Joint arrangements and machinery develop. Some of the difficult problems separating the parties are solved by workable compromises, thus reducing the core of conflict. Long-term agreements and negotiated pensions are further evidence of a settled relationship. In other words, accommodation tends to take place.

In essence, the bargaining process is part conflict and part cooperation for the purpose of arriving at solutions to problems. In its early years, the union and its leadership may have stressed hostility toward the employer and even toward the capitalistic system. But with continued joint dealing and successful negotiation, psychological changes are prone to occur on both sides.

In many situations, emotional maturity, with recognition of mutual interests in problem-solving, have caused radical union sentiments and rugged employer opposition to subside. Three or four decades ago American unions were more diverse in aims and operations than is the case today. For instance, the Industrial Workers of the World, which flourished before World War I, was violently anti-capitalistic and, therefore, did not believe in negotiated agreements. Successful experience with bargaining has reduced differences among unions, as practical operation has submerged ideology. Nowadays the demands of unions are similar, and their written agreements contain the same type of provisions, whether they deal with union security, seniority, or grievance procedures ending in arbitration.

On the employer side, experience seems to have demonstrated to many corporate managements that unionism does not constitute a basic threat to their security. When unions are really accepted by management, a shift in company objectives and perspectives in labor relations tends to take place. Both sides think in longer-run terms and gain in respect for one another.[10] Collaborative aspects of the relationship play a more significant role. Under such circumstances, three developments are likely to occur. They are: (1) increasing professionalization of the bargaining process, (2) more attention on administration and enforcement of the agreement, and (3) less use of the strike weapon.

As experience with collective bargaining accumulates, the process, for various reasons, becomes more professional. In the first place, the subjects treated in negotiations are increasingly technical. They have come to include pensions, medical and hospital care, supplementary unemployment benefits, scientific management, and additional legal requirements. Consequently, both in the formulation of union demands and in negotiations concerning them, both sides put considerable reliance on technicians and experts. In the second place, negotiations concerned with time-honored subjects like wages now call for a fairly high level of statistical sophistication and knowledge of national patterns. In the third place, both sides are prone to present their best "team" for negotiations, and those with the most practice and superior knowledge on the union side are generally the full-time union officials. The centralizing tendencies already discussed and any movement from plant to company-wide or multi-employer bargaining also help to concentrate collective bargaining, like professional sports, in the hands of full-time specialists or professionals.

A natural result of continued negotiations and successful collective bargaining is that a greater proportion of time and effort, particularly on the union side, are devoted to administering and enforcing the agreement. Partly that is because the time interval between negotiations tends to lengthen and agreements grow larger and more detailed. Partly also it is because labor organizations gradually assume greater responsibilities and seek to establish themselves as businesslike and well-disciplined institutions. Indeed, some writers have pointed out that unions have been taking over a portion of management's disciplinary functions, such as the elimination of wildcat strikes and enforcement of work rules embodied in the agreement. In a sense, the union is part owner of the agreement and, therefore, has an interest in protecting its property from infringement.

The use and character of the strike has also altered in many union-management relationships. As relations continue, resort to striking is likely to be less frequent, and any strikes generally are less severe or emotional. The lockout has fallen into even greater disuse. All this is understandable. With repeated negotiation of new agreements, the issues sharply separating the parties are compromised and new employee rights become established. Subsequent negotiations are less likely to involve a challenge to the rights and security of either party. Furthermore, the parties come to know one another better and become more skilled in negotiations. With increasing professionalization, the negotiations are more intelligent, reasoned, and moderate.[11] One does not need to subscribe to the theory that strikes result principally from miscalculation by one party or both[12] in order to understand why less emotion and more thoughtful search for solutions reduces strike propensities. Then too, the professionals and top leaders on both sides, for reasons of prestige and tenure, have a personal interest in peaceful settlements. The "managements" of both companies and unions find that agreements without strikes make their work easier and improve their reputations in the community.

The amiable character of many present-day strikes in large firms is explained not only by changed attitudes but also by environmental conditions. It is, of course, increasingly difficult for unions to picture managements of large corporations as ogres or even as unenlightened, and much the same is true of any attempt to portray most unions as anti-capitalistic or revolutionary in aim and intent. Undoubtedly, full employment and price inflation have contributed to a relaxed management view toward industrial disputes. But public opinion has also played a role. A general feeling exists that something is wrong with the leadership if settlements cannot be negotiated without an extended strike. A severe work stoppage injures the prestige of leaders on both sides. Any theory of the strike needs to take account of incentives to the maintenance of good relations, including the leadership's desire to avoid damage to the institution's and their leader's public reputations.

What are the implications of these three developments? Is it natural for collective bargaining to move in the direction of emotional maturity, bargaining proficiency, and emphasis on administrative and enforcement activities? Does the bargaining process tend to develop specialization and centralization, understanding and responsibility, and attenuation of the strike weapon? Does collective bargaining have a taming effect?

Undoubtedly, a succession of settlements contributes to a long-run tendency for union-management relations to settle down to a more mild and institutionalized operation. Even the pageantry of skilled professionals matching wits cannot conceal the fact that the actual rate of innovation is declining and that a maturity of relationships has developed. True, there are exceptions to the settling-down process, especially where the environment is uncongenial to unionism, as in small-town and rural areas in sections of the South and mid-West. Collective bargaining does generate conflict, particularly if one side or the other poses as defender of a past faith —whether early individualism, fanatical unionism, or a radical political ideology. Labor relations in such an environment are inclined to be unstable. Eventually either one party is eliminated or viewpoints are modified and moderated. With sufficient time, adjustment is inherent in the negotiating process.

Collective bargaining, of course, is too dynamic and adaptive to have an ultimate stage. Its processes can be used for a variety of purposes and its results are manifold. Nevertheless, some general tendencies appear evident from experience during the past two decades. Extended bargaining experience, relatively free from government intervention, does seem to develop trends toward professionalization of the process, toward increased responsibility and businesslike dealing, and toward less industrial strife.

Collective Bargaining in the Future

Can one project these trends into the future? Are they so basic that they are likely to continue henceforth without being reversed?

Much, of course, will depend on developments within

American management. Conceivably a widespread campaign could develop to reduce union effectiveness in collective bargaining. That, however, seems unlikely. Management and union leaders have learned the advantages of good relations, of the quick and effective settlement of grievances, and of the application of advances in psychology to industrial relations problems. Moreover, collective bargaining develops governmental rules and machinery, including no-strike clauses and enforcement by arbitration if necessary. The industrial government jointly established can penalize the parties for infraction of the rules. Such disciplinary arrangements are advantageous to management, rendering worker rebellions more and more difficult.

Unions obviously have a great stake in good labor-management relations. Collective bargaining is their program and their chief business. A union can achieve security and normal growth by gaining and maintaining the respect and good will of managements within its jurisdiction. With the pioneering possibilities reduced and differences in worklife and in life patterns diminished, it is understandable that unions, for the most part, have become more businesslike in their aims and operations. Possessing a good understanding of the realities in the situation, the leadership on each side can play its role, fully aware of the futility of inflexibility. In a sense, both sides are trying to satisfy the employees—to minimize their discontent and gain their consent to the conditions of employment. That common objective provides much of the mutuality of interest in collective bargaining.

In view of recent and prospective developments, collective bargaining appears destined to proceed, in the main, along the lines followed during the past decade. There seems little likelihood, for example, of a long-run shift away from professionalization toward decentralization of negotiations or away from reasoned and businesslike dealing toward greater reliance on emotion and the strike weapon.

Nevertheless, as is true of union development, the path of experience does not conform rigidly to long-run tendencies. Short-run shifts and variations are to be expected. Each negotiating unit has a separate history of collective bargaining, and such historical differences contribute to current diversity. But if the above analysis is valid, the direction of the general movement appears definite, and the forces that have been responsible for the broad developments in collective bargaining in this country during the recent past seem likely to be dominant, at least over the next decade.

There has been an assumption that collective bargaining in the United States would more or less follow patterns developed in other democratic countries, like England and Sweden, in which unions became well established and accepted by management much earlier than here. However, distinctly American developments make any close conformity unlikely.

National negotiations covering a whole industry are a case in point. In England and Sweden the dominant pattern has been such industry-wide bargaining between national unions and employers associations. The leading role of large firms in American mass-production industries and their industrial relations philosophies and staffs make any such pattern unlikely here. About two-thirds of workers covered by labor agreements in this country are under those negotiated on a plant or single-company basis, and only one-fifth are under agreements negotiated nationally or regionally on a multi-company basis. In fact, during the decade after World War II, multi-employer agreements on a national or regional basis probably declined in terms of the percentage of all workers covered by union-management contracts who were under national and regional contracts.

On the other hand, the scope of bargaining is much wider

in the United States than in Britain or Sweden. Partly that has been due to the predominance of company negotiations in this country. Company differentiation has permitted more experimentation here, even though long-run forces may recently have had a dampening effect on pioneering under collective bargaining in America. Other factors differentiating our experience from theirs have been a greater degree of union rivalry here, less solidarity of bargaining policy, and less central federation influence on bargaining demands.

Such contrasts could be pursued further. The important point, however, is that the methods, scope, and philosophy of collective bargaining in a country are influenced by its industrial and union structures and by historical developments. And long-run trends in bargaining relationships may operate differently or be modified significantly, depending on the country's institutional and cultural setting.

This chapter has attempted to set forth the long-run trends in collective bargaining in the United States. They include greater centralization and professionalization, more business-like conduct and stress on administration, and less diversification and use of the strike to achieve objectives. In general, these trends seem likely to continue, or at least not to be reversed, during the next decade. Developments in collective bargaining here are governed more by past experience and American conditions than they are by any pattern of prior evolution abroad or any supposedly universal trends.

XI. IMPLICATIONS FOR ECONOMIC
ANALYSIS

THE THEORY OF UNION BEHAVIOR is not far advanced. Systematic speculation concerning unionism is still at a fairly elementary stage. Attempts to apply in the labor field modes of analysis developed and refined elsewhere have not proved too rewarding. Few have been the secrets of trade unionism that have yielded to such systems of alien logic.

Among the social scientists, economists have been particularly prone to apply their well-cultivated doctrines to the area of industrial relations. Often they begin by assuming that unions must seek to maximize something. Reasoning from the theory of the firm and from consumer economics, they naturally start with an assumption of maximization and are, of course, partial to quantities measurable in money. The late Professor Henry C. Simons apparently assumed that unions would seek to maximize the life-time earnings of the present membership of the union.[1] After considering various candidates for the goal of union activity, Professor John T. Dunlop selected the largest total income for the then current membership (wage scales multiplied by employment, plus unemployment benefits collected by the membership) as the most appropriate magnitude.[2] Professor Selig Perlman seems to put monopoly control of job opportunities as the main union objective.[3]

Others, eschewing purely economic interpretations, have attempted to define union aims more broadly—often in terms of "welfare" of the membership or institutional security and growth in membership. However, as Professor

[127]

Arthur M. Ross points out, the problem of defining even "*economic* welfare" is most difficult. It includes a "congeries of discrete phenomena—wages, with a dollar dimension; hours of work, with a time dimension; and physical working conditions, economic security, protection against managerial abuse,"[4] and so forth. The more heterogeneous and nebulous the assumed objective, the greater is the variety of actions and programs which can be defended as pursuing that purpose. A single, simple aim facilitates rigor in formulation and manipulation but may prove grossly insufficient or mostly irrelevant.

Chapter 1 indicated the shortcomings of attempts to interpret American unionism by means of a static or mechanistic type of theory, which pretends to offer universally applicable generalizations. The burden of this book has been that, with respect to labor organizations and labor relations, such theorizing is inadequate for many significant questions and problems. Unions undergo an internal metamorphosis, and the circumstances to which they adapt do and will alter. Consequently, an evolutionary theory of unionism is needed —one that takes account of changes through time and that relates its generalizations to particular settings. It is important to know why unions today differ from the same unions twenty or fifty years ago, why American unions are unlike their counterparts (say) in England or Egypt, and how our union movement is likely to develop over the next decade or two. Answers to such questions can be supplied only by study of the form of trade unionism that has been developing in this country and of trends in the American labor movement.

Theory of the Union

Throughout our analysis, the importance of institutional development over time has been stressed. Change explains why a theoretical construct designed for the early phases of unionism, when it is in the crusading and conquest period, may need to be significantly modified for later, more mature stages of evolution.

Previous chapters have examined some of the ways in which the objectives and operations of American unions have altered during recent decades. The purpose was to analyze evolutionary change rather than to develop a systematic theory of union behavior. Nevertheless a study of trends does have implications for a short-run theory of unionism.

In the first place, the broadening of objectives, particularly on the part of the leadership, is a development of importance for theorizing about union behavior. As already explained, such widening of perspectives is tied up with the achievement of some goals and with increased integration of unions into the community. The changing nature of the employment relationship—its humanizing, the expansion in welfare and tenure obligations, and the elimination of work-term differences between manual and salaried employees—has helped to alter the role that unions play in industry. The same is true of the routinization of many union processes, such as organization of new employees and dues collection under agreements providing for the union shop and the check-off. Moreover, greater stability, responsibility, and integration have, in many unions, been accompanied by corrupting as well as moderating influences. A theory applicable to American unionism must encompass these developmental factors.

The changing character of collective bargaining is another important consideration in systematic theorizing about union behavior. As the subject matter of negotiations changes, so does the role of the expert in union affairs. As the philosophies and policies of the parties alter, so do union tactics and the use of understanding and restraint in the negotiating sessions. A theory of union behavior should elucidate the respective roles of reason, emotion, and politics in union affairs. When union negotiating rights are gained by governmental certification and the arbitration of unsettled grievances is almost universal, adaptations occur in the union and in the use of the strike. The more labor rules are adopted by government action or by joint agreement, the more unions tend to be legal- and enforcement-minded and the less prone they are to strike. Any atrophy of the strike has important implications for the theory of the union.

Chapter v contained a discussion of unions as "sleepy monopolies." Perhaps a more appropriate term would be "integrated maturity." It is not so much that unions and their leadership become characterized simply by inertia, contentment, and desire for an easy life. Rather they change somewhat in their objectives and methods. A term like "integrated maturity" gives some recognition to the positive factors of development, adaptation, and assimilation.

Furthermore, sections of a union may not develop equally or along parallel lines. For example, the national leadership may mature more rapidly than parts of the membership, in which case the union is faced with internal problems of political compromise. The leadership may think in terms of a program of union education as a means of developing more harmony of viewpoint within the organization. In any event, the rate and character of metamorphosis in the various levels and parts of the union organization are significant considerations for a theory of trade unionism.

Since the 1920's, the political aspects of American unionism seem to have become more dominant. A number of factors apparently help to explain the increased influence of political considerations, using "political" in the broad sense of that term. The Wagner Act and particularly the Taft-Hartley Act have stressed elections for certification and other purposes. Undoubtedly the broadening of union activities and increased government control of industrial relations have played a part. Another factor has been the expanded role of the union federations, which clearly are political organizations whose primary purpose is to protect the interests of labor in Washington, in the states, and in municipalities. Perhaps the entrenchment of union political machines has been still another factor. Such entrenchment has enlarged the latitude for noneconomic considerations in union policy-determination and operation.

In Chapter II the similarities between unions and political parties were mentioned. Developments in recent decades appear to have accentuated the common characteristics of these two types of organization. As already explained, the internal processes of unions are political. Balloting is the ultimate method of decision-making. Much of the time of union officials is taken up with internal politics—including the development of a political machine—and with national, state, and local politics. As unions age, a higher percentage of the time of the organization tends to be devoted to personal grievances and benefits, and even greater stress is placed on loyalty to the organization and its leadership.

As experience accumulates and as the gulf between unions and employers narrows, labor relations seem to move closer to the sort of relationship that exists between the Republican and Democratic Parties. Although political parties are cast in the role of opponents, they cooperate in various activities including the legislative process. Similarly, unions and managements cooperate in plant affairs and even in the negotiation of new agreements, if one considers constructive compromise to be part of cooperation. Bargaining is frequently an important element in the legislative process under a two-party system, just as collective bargaining is a form of legislation designed to achieve acceptance of terms by a constituency. Union conventions often resemble political conventions, and the processes of drafting programs or platforms in both types of organization are not too dissimilar. Indeed, the periodic convention is a key element in the structure of both unions and political parties.

Although the factors influencing the evolution of labor organizations and political parties are not identical, unions in their operations are obviously closer to political parties than they are to business enterprises. Consequently, the theory of union behavior should ultimately extract more sustenance from political theory than it has been able to draw from economic models based on the theory of the firm.

What implications do the above-mentioned developments have for the theory of union behavior? If union activities broaden in scope, if the horizons of union leaders widen and lengthen, if union functions and powers become more centralized, and if the central federation assumes a more significant role in union affairs, surely the objectives of unions are likely to undergo some alteration. The character and outlook of unions may also change with increased stress on rulemaking and rule enforcement and with less resort to the strike weapon.

The problem is how to integrate developmental change into union theory. At least three courses of action are possible. One is to be content with a loose, framework type of theory, which makes no pretense at prediction. It assumes that unions differ from one another and from time to time, and provides for the classification of factors and thus an orderly means for explaining such differences. Another approach would be to work out a theory of the union behavior separately for each stage of union development. That might mean, for example, "job-conscious" unionism of the Perlman type to apply to craft unionism prior to the Great Depression; a broad-gauge, reformist model of unionism to apply to organizations like Reuther's United Automobile Workers in the past and the immediate future; and a broad-scope yet cooperative model to apply to the more settled situation like that of the Amalgamated Clothing Workers since World War II.

A third approach would be to develop a theory of union evolution as an all-embracing theory of union behavior. That seems to be the position of Professor Hubert Brochier of the University of Grenoble, France.[5] He would bring union structural, historical, and growth considerations into one general theory of union action.

At this early stage in thinking about union evolution, it seems premature to select one of these as the preferred approach. The third, single-theory view has the greatest intellectual appeal but obviously is confronted with difficult problems of integration and explanation of developmental variations.

Wage Theory

Union and collective-bargaining developments have not been well integrated into wage theory. The influence of union evolution upon wage structures and levels is still largely an unexplored area. However, various data seem to indicate that significant relationships do exist between wages and union ageing.

In this connection, two types of wage material are instructive. One type apparently indicates that youthful unionism (the early organizational stage) is more potent wage-wise than mature unionism. Two statistical studies for this country, one covering the period from 1890 to 1926 and the other from 1933 to 1946, seem to show that new unionism is a source of relative wage advantage and that, wage-wise, settled unionism may be a restraining factor.[6] The second study, for example, revealed that the group of six industries substantially organized in 1933 and remaining so, lagged behind all other groups in increase in hourly earnings, even behind those industries that continued to be unorganized.

The second type of material does not lend itself so well to direct comparisons. It consists of miscellaneous evidence that unions in this country and abroad have not pressed for wage increases as high as economic conditions warranted. Abroad employers have voluntarily granted additions to the negotiated increases, which in Sweden and England have come to be known as "wage drift." As explained in Chapter vii, a study of actual earnings and negotiated rates in England for the period 1938 to 1955 indicated that one-fifth of the increase in earnings could be accounted for only by rates or payments in excess of the nationally-bargained rates.[7] In Sweden the wage drift appears to have been responsible for two-fifths of the increase in manual workers' earnings from 1939 to 1955.[8] In other words, for labor supply and other reasons in particular industries, employers raised their wage scales progressively above the nationally bargained rates. The unions failed in their official bargaining to negotiate wages as high as many employers were able and willing to pay.

A similar wage drift undoubtedly has occurred in some of the piece-rate industries in this country, for their earnings have been creeping upwards more than bargained increases alone would warrant. However, the time rates negotiated in industries like autos and steel are the standard (not the minimum) rates and, therefore, the negotiated scales are not exceeded as has been so widely the case in Sweden and England. Nevertheless, some evidence exists that the prices, and also presumably the labor costs, of manufacturing firms in oligopolistic or administered price lines have, at times, lagged behind the full market-justified figures.[9]

The broadening of union objectives also has implications for wage theory. It means less stress on wages alone and more on other elements of compensation in "package settlements." The substitution of benefits of various types for (say) the equivalent amount of wage increase raises a number of interesting issues for both wage theory and economic theory.

Unions have an influence on the form of employee compensation and the uses of labor income. Through collective bargaining, they help to determine not only the distribution between wage and non-wage compensation but also the division among the various types of "fringe" or non-wage components. It is in the non-wage area that the question of coercive purchase has arisen and that a conflict between individual and collective determination of the spending of employee compensation sometimes occurs. Established on a group basis, negotiated benefit programs automatically apply to all workers in the bargaining unit.

Generally, unions as institutions can gain more credit, security, and prestige from negotiated benefits, which represent a specific purchase, than they would from an equivalent rise in money wages, which constitute generalized purchasing power. The establishment of a new benefit, such as supplemental unemployment compensation, is a breakthrough by collective bargaining, which the union can claim would not have been achieved in the absence of labor organization. To the union as an institution, benefit programs have the advantage that they increase its functions by developing new areas in which the union comes to represent the members' interests. They place the organization in the position of buying agent for the family with power to decide problems of allocation. The union, in turn, can point to the economical purchases made through the method of group buying under collective bargaining. Benefit programs may place organized labor in a position to be courted by insurance companies and other financial institutions, while at the same time giving wage-earners some of the advantages and status of salaried employees.

Various statistical studies show that supplemental compensation, particularly negotiated benefit programs, has increased in significance relative to wages during the past two decades. For instance, non-wage compensation is estimated to have risen from 6 per cent of labor cost in this country in 1938 to 14 per cent in 1951.[10] Another survey indicates that hourly earnings in American industry rose but 54 per cent in the decade from 1947 to 1957, while fringe benefits rose by some 133 per cent.[11] In short, negotiated benefit programs have represented a progressively larger percentage of employee compensation during the past twenty years and that trend seems likely to continue—at least for the next few years.

This remarkable rise in supplemental compensation relative to money earnings can hardly be explained by the market mechanism and the marginal productivity theory. Based on individual and incremental purchases, those old reliables of the economics textbooks are weak intellectual instruments for interpreting the recent growth, the levels, and the limits, of bargained benefits. Part of the explanation certainly must be in terms of the union as an institution with broadening objectives.

Without doubt unions are partly responsible for the allocation of an increasing proportion of payroll costs devoted to fringe benefits.[12] A 1956 study, based on extensive interviews with union and management officials in the Boston metropolitan area, found that the prevailing view among both union leaders and employers was that most of the rank-and-file members would prefer direct wage increases to an equivalent amount used for the purchase of employee benefits.[13] Those interviewed, for the most part, credited unions and their leaders with "selling" fringe benefits to the rank-and-file by all sorts of methods. As the author explains:

Throughout the many conversations, it was of great interest to note the union officials' conceptual analyses of the process of fringe coercion [persuasion plus influence]. A majority of them affirmed the belief that given an absolute alternative between a straight ten-cent increase and a package of five cents in fringes and five cents in wages, the workmen will disapprove the latter and almost unanimously approve the former. That the union ultimately accepted the package was attributed by many to their own capacities for the exercise of successful leadership. Thus, although short-sightedness prevailed among the rank and file, the officials, by exercise of proper leadership, never submitted such an absolute alternative and hence never had to fear the shortsightedness nor face the possibility of disapproval.[14]

The institutional factors in the process of collective decision-making have been largely neglected in economic theory.

Clearly the many facets of non-wage compensation need to be explored and integrated with wage theory and economic analysis. As they have evolved, American unions have been exercising more and more allocative functions with respect to forms of compensation and the spending or investing of funds. The growth of non-wage compensation raises a host of questions pertinent to the problems of labor cost and price inflation as well as wage theory. On net balance, has the increasing proportion of non-wage compensation been an inflationary or a deflationary factor, or has its influence varied in direction from time to time? Have fringe benefits partly served as a sort of "non-wage drift," because they, better than wage scales, can be adjusted to the relative ability of companies and industries to meet labor costs? What effects have the trends in labor development previously discussed had on wage structures and wage levels? Will the centralizing tendencies begin to jump the sharp dividing line between the national unions and the AFL-CIO not only with respect to the issue of ethical practices but also with respect to union wage policy, along the lines of developments in England, Sweden, and other European countries? Such questions indicate some of the wage implications of any investigation of union development.

Furthermore, trade unions in America, by expanding the

non-wage aspects of the terms and conditions of work, have been one of the principal factors in replacing the commodity concept of employment with a social welfare conception of the employer-employee relationship. The welfare concept encompasses not only employee grievance protections, tenure rights, and employee benefits, but also ethical notions and dignified treatment included under the heading, "human relations."

During the past half century a revolution has occurred in the dimensions of manual employment, especially in the larger firms. Before World War I plant employees, particu-larly in bigger companies, were regarded with what Cyrus Ching has referred to as "a sort of calloused indifference to their plight."[15] They were hired and dismissed with little notion of any employer obligation or employee rights in a job. As late as the 1920's, it was customary in the automobile industry, with a model change, to close the plant, to pay off the men, and then to rehire them as starting employees when employment picked up.[16] Now unions even negotiate higher pension benefits for previously retired employees as well as insurance protection for retirees and their dependents.

Many factors in addition to unions and collective bargain-ing help to account for the new features that have been added to the terms and conditions of employment. Among the other factors that have helped to shift employment from a commercial transaction to a welfare relationship have been the following: the higher educational level of the work force, the curtailment of immigration, the much larger capital in-vestment per employee in industry, new developments in applied psychology, the trend toward professionalization of management, and changes in public opinion as levels of liv-ing have risen. Of course, alterations in the employment concept have gone much further in the larger firms than in most of the smaller ones, and much further in some indus-tries such as oil and autos than in others like longshoring and building construction. Indeed, as Lloyd Fisher so well explained, the commodity concept continues in almost pure form in the impersonal, anonymous treatment of harvest hands in a state like California.[17]

The development of codes of proper employment practice has, as indicated in Chapter IV, had an influence on union evolution. The discussion in Chapter V indicated that unions have, by improving employment standards, tended to diminish the opportunities for further expansion of the scope of bargaining—the possibilities of adding more new dimensions to the employment relationship. Nevertheless, some further evolution in the employment concept is likely to occur in large firms, as living standards and the social sciences advance and as further redefinition of decent and proper treatment of employees takes place, especially for older and retired workers.

While practice has been making great strides forward, theory has tended to stand still. Economists, for instance, have been slow to adjust their thinking to the notable changes in the dimensions and facets of employment. They have been prone to continue to think in commodity terms, to talk of "the labor market" and "the competitive" or "equilibrium wage," as though wages now play the same role that they did before World War I and as though the new aspects of the employment relationship can be disregarded in economic analysis.[18]

The changes both in unions and in the concept of employment have implications for wage theory that so far have, for the most part, remained unexplored. Of course, these changes also have important implications for economic growth through their effects on consumption patterns, on investment funds, and on management efficiency; but those ramifications cannot be pursued here. The purpose of this chapter has been to indicate that theoretical speculation concerning union behavior and wages should not neglect the evolutionary process in unions, especially in an economy in which some sixteen to eighteen million workers are covered by collective-bargaining agreements and thirteen million employees and their families are under negotiated benefit plans.[19]

XII. IMPLICATIONS FOR
PUBLIC POLICY

A THEORY OF UNION EVOLUTION raises significant questions for public policy, including labor relations legislation. Should the government promote, oppose, or be neutral toward the long-run tendencies and trends in organized labor? Should the developmental drift be encouraged, resisted, or modified?

From an evolutionary viewpoint, a law that is appropriate for one stage in the development of a country's labor movement may be ill-suited for an earlier or subsequent stage. In the early years of union development, legislation may be necessary in order to protect the right to organize and to bargain, if in that country an independent labor movement is to exist and function effectively. Also, in the formative stage, the government may be able to exert a significant influence on the character and structure of the labor movement. After union structures have been long embedded in a complex of institutional practice, any statutory program for, say, union decentralization or structural reform may be doomed to fail because it comes so late in the evolutionary development of unionism in that country.

Following the spread of organization but before union-management relations have settled down, there may be a period when the parties seem to be divided by fundamental differences in industrial relations philosophy and when major tests of strength reflect such differences. Under those circumstances, government intervention in the collective bargaining process may be difficult to avoid, and legislation may be passed setting up all sorts of settlement procedures including mediation, fact-finding, and arbitration. Later on, when relations have matured and the core of conflict separating the parties has considerably contracted, restrictions on the right to strike can be relaxed or eliminated, and legislative guarantees of organizational and bargaining rights may be superfluous except possibly in areas of potential union expansion.

In reflecting on the role of government at the present stage in the evolution of American unionism, it should be borne in mind (1) that labor organizations and union-management relations have experienced a process of maturing and (2) that the centralizing tendencies in American unionism have been developing over a long period of time. The maturing or accommodating process has resulted in the practical elimination of class warfare in America. As a consequence, recent years have witnessed a widespread consensus concerning basic economic issues, such as ownership of the means of production, the economic policies of the Federal Government, social security, and the role of employee benefit programs. Both sides have been interested in expanding the concept of employment, although they may differ with respect to particular dimensions or emphasis.

Altered conditions have tended to shift the nature of any need for legislative action. With increasing union-management accommodation under union shop agreements, with growing membership apathy for lack of emotional involvement, and with greater size and machine control of unions, stress may need to be placed on the protection of the democratic rights and civil rights of individual members within the organization. In other words, the evolution of unions may have given a new urgency to the problem of individual rights and protections—an urgency which has been recognized by the AFL-CIO in adopting codes of ethical and proper union practice.

At this stage of union evolution, some fundamental thinking is required if we are to have intelligent consideration of legislative proposals for union reform. We need to ask ourselves such questions as the following: Should Federal legislation and its administration try to strengthen the moderating influences within unions, or should they stimulate employers to challenge union rights and even a union's security? Should the government encourage union unity, or seek to nurture interunion and intra-union rivalry and to enlarge any gaps between the national leadership and the membership? Should public policy foster union centralizing tendencies, or should it aim at strengthening democratic checks within unions, even to the extent of requiring that all bargaining be on a strictly local basis? Should the government aid or resist the tendency for the central federation to acquire more influence? Should legislation seek to promote the integration of unions into the community, or to separate them by special statutory controls applicable to unions only? Should it encourage the tendency for unions to become a part of society's disciplinary machinery, promoting contract observance and orderly procedures, or should the government encourage employer challenges to unions that may cause them to refrain from accepting such responsibilities?

As these questions imply, the Federal Government should have some sort of conscious policy toward evolutionary trends. And the government's policy, whether contained in legislation or administrative action, ought to be as consistent as possible in its objectives, so that its recommendations do not seem to aim in all directions.

Role of the State

People differ widely in their views concerning the appropriate degree of governmental regulation of unions and labor-management relations. Those who take a firm stand in favor of reduced government control and curtailed Federal powers often, without much consistency, advocate detailed Federal regulation of unions and labor agreements.

And union leaders frequently insist on the desirability of a hands-off policy for the state in the case of union affairs, while at the same time they propose further Federal intervention in business. Commonly, self-interest seems to preclude consistency of personal philosophy regarding labor and other parts of the economy.

One philosophy of unionism would seek to reduce the influence and power of the national organization. Under proposed legislative action, national unions would be curtailed by such means as the following: have certification (the one-year bargaining franchise granted by the NLRB) held only by local unions, forbid all national or regional bargaining on a multi-employer basis, require government-supervised strike votes, and ban any union security provisions under so-called "right-to-work" laws.

While such reforms might weaken some unions, others would be invigorated by the challenge. For example, experience indicates that strike votes conducted by government provide an occasion for union campaigns to arouse the membership and also may stimulate leadership resentment, because one of their purposes is to drive a wedge between the membership and the hierarchy.[1] Prohibition of union security, by forcing unions to spend additional time and resources on organization and dues collection, would serve to keep the leadership more conscious of rank-and-file discontent and cause it to prosecute more grievances of questionable validity. Although perhaps unappreciated by their advocates, such measures would tend to lessen the willingness of national union officials to help enforce agreements. As Professor Sumner H. Slichter has emphasized, conditions in this country have made the national union the key unit in the structure of American unionism.[2] A weakening of that unit would reduce union responsibility.

For more than a century prior to World War II, American unions were unable to organize their jurisdictions and to keep them organized. Nonunion competition was an ever-present threat to their existence. Consequently, unions in this country have inherited a traditional sense of insecurity that seems to affect many of their leaders even today, despite increased stability and security of the organization. That concern undoubtedly helps to explain the vigor with which organized labor attacks "right-to-work" laws, even though they are widely disregarded and remain unenforced. It also underlies union denunciations of the free-speech provisions and other encouragements of employer opposition to organization that are contained in the Taft-Hartley Act as currently interpreted.

Advocates of legislation designed to reconstruct American unionism might well ponder the probable effects of their proposals upon union stability and maturity. They might ask themselves whether they wish to bring about more intra-union and interunion rivalry, whether they want to stir unions by challenges that will increase their militancy and reduce their responsibility. If they do not desire to reverse union evolution, moving back toward the conditions of organized labor in the 1930's, they should explain how, or the extent to which, their recommendations would avoid such a result.

Another, and different, type of labor philosophy is that which favors laissez-faire or government abstention, except for the certification of bargaining agents and a legal duty to bargain in good faith. Reliance is placed on the values of collective bargaining and on the evolutionary process in unions and in labor-management relations. The assumption is that both unions and labor relations will mature sooner and better without government regulation of the bargaining process or its results. Special legislation may be needed to defend certification from jurisdictional disputes, to protect innocent third parties from pressure to participate in a boycott, or to safeguard the public in the rare case of a real emergency strike. Beyond that, the parties should be left free to work out their own solutions and destiny. Faith is placed on the processes of self-settlement, leading to rules and routines, grievance precedents, and patterns of industrial practice.

An example of this philosophy is contained in the 1954 Report to the Governor by a special Committee on the Public Utility Disputes Act in New Jersey.[3] David L. Cole, well known arbitrator and former head of the Federal Mediation and Conciliation Service, served as the Commission's chairman. In recommending outright repeal of a 1946 law (last amended in 1950) under which utility disputes declared by the Governor to be an emergency are subject to compulsory arbitration, the majority made the point that trust should be placed in the sense of responsibility of the parties and in the bargaining process as the sound solution in the long run.

Promotion of established trends in American unionism would be a third philosophical position. Presumably such encouragement would be mainly by administrative action and moral suasion, although certain legislation could be helpful in advancing union stability and maturity.

Some illustrations will indicate the implications of this philosophy. The appointment of union officials to advisory or policy boards in government would be a way of fostering wider interests and union integration. Another means of furthering past evolutionary tendencies would be by the encouragement of arbitration and long-term agreements, by improving arbitration laws and panels, and by providing good statistical series on the cost of living and productivity. The Federal Administration could also use its influence in favor of labor unity and centralization, namely, by lending prestige to the merged AFL-CIO at the national level. In that connection, legislation might provide Federal support for the ethical, financial, and democratic standards of the AFL-CIO by incorporating such standards into a statute and providing that, where appropriate private means of determination and enforcement were not in operation, procedures under Federal auspices would apply. Thus, it would not be possible for unions, either by expulsion from the AFL-CIO or by absence of affiliation, to avoid its codes of good union conduct. Various other actions by government could also serve to promote union stability, responsibility, and maturity.

There is, of course, no one correct philosophy of government toward unions. The kind of union movement one desires depends on his personal value judgments, which, in turn, are often influenced by his position in the economy. Study of past trends and future probabilities may enable one better to understand the forces behind change. It cannot, however, determine personal goals nor alter self-interests. One can, nevertheless, hope for intelligent assessment of patterns and some internal consistency in the public policies that particular persons support in the labor field.

Above all, study of evolutionary change should provide one with some appreciation of the difficulties of attempting to turn back the clock, of trying to wipe out by legislation developments that have become well established for a decade or longer. And governmental attempts to reverse union evolution piecemeal encounter the problem that individual trends are generally part of a whole network of development. This is not to say that government is powerless in the labor area, but only that politics is the art of achieving the possible and that the possibilities are greater if one works with the pattern of evolution rather than against the stream of developments, especially when dealing with a movement composed of eighteen million workers.

Some Crucial Issues

An evolutionary viewpoint on unions and union-management relations serves to highlight certain crucial questions and dilemmas that confront lawmakers in the labor field.

Briefly stated, four of these issues are as follows: (1) variation and experimentation *vs.* national conformity and uniformity, (2) responsibility of the labor movement for union democracy and members' rights *vs.* governmental machinery and operation for those purposes, (3) union responsibility for ethical standards and their enforcement *vs.* governmentally imposed and enforced standards, and (4) independence of the labor movement *vs.* partial domination and direction by the state.

In a sense these four issues are but aspects of the larger question: To what extent should unions be permitted to determine their own evolution and how far should the government intervene to control change in this area? Where should the balance be drawn between unions as private, voluntary institutions and unions as certified bargaining agents clothed with a public interest, which the government has a duty to protect even though that may necessitate deep penetration into the internal affairs of labor organizations? Although the four issues overlap and are encompassed within this broader question, it may be helpful to examine each of them separately.

Blanket legislation at the Federal level, especially if it involves detailed regulation, may serve to straitjacket development and to deprive unions of their adaptability and vitality. Largely on its own initiative, organized labor has developed along the lines already discussed, with each national union determining its own policies under a tradition of autonomy. In a country with such diversified industry and employment practices, flexibility to adjust to environmental conditions and changes is a real virtue. Freedom to develop has enabled American trade unionism to become better integrated into the larger society.

Adjustment to the times and to developing standards is one reason why it is desirable to rely heavily on the corrective influence of public opinion and on organized labor to formulate and enforce its own codes of proper conduct. That sort of viewpoint leads to stress on such statutory measures as requirements for union reporting and disclosure of the facts rather than on legal compulsions imposed in a punitive spirit upon a movement with eighteen million members. In any attempt at general union reform or restructuring, a big problem is that of enforcement, which may be so difficult or lax as to encourage widespread disregard and disrespect for the law.

The second issue, that of internal democracy and protection of individuals' rights within the union, is even more complex and troublesome. Democracy cannot simply be imposed from without; it must develop within and depends largely on the spirit, tradition, and willingness of the members to participate. Nevertheless, the government can provide a framework of rules and standards that will help to facilitate the preservation and growth of democratic processes and checks.

As American unions have evolved, the need for such a supporting framework has increased. It is true that no sharp break has occurred in the democratic tradition and professions of American unionism. Union constitutions, for the most part, still approach the democratic ideal. National unions have always lacked some of the protective elements of political democracy. By and large, they have had one-party (rather than two political party) government, with the union periodical controlled by the incumbent administration and without the safeguards to the individual member of a truly independent judiciary. Nevertheless, developments in recent decades have both added and subtracted elements of union control that are significant for the democratic process.

Some of these altered conditions and factors have been explained in previous chapters. Unions have become more centralized and more businesslike and orderly. The reduction of rival unionism, the decline in internal factionalism, and greater control over locals by the national headquarters have made it more difficult to challenge the existing administration. That is so not only because of the potential cost and delay involved in pursuing a claim of improper or unconstitutional action, but also because of the difficulties and disfavor with fellow unionists that are caused by bringing a court complaint against the union's administration.

One big difference from the pre-1930's era is the added fact of NLRB certification of a union as the sole and exclusive bargaining agent for *all* the employees in the bargaining unit. That very action involves not only a monopoly of representation rights and an implied stamp of approval for the union by the government, but also carries with it some supposition that all who are represented by the union in that unit should have a right to participate in the choice of officers and in the determination of policies by the certified union. With certification, the union is presumed to be representative government.

But that presumption need not mean a government-sponsored campaign to enforce union democracy or even union elections conducted by the government. Indeed, government-run elections for the officers and convention delegates of 77,000 locals and for national officials and convention ballots, would be a costly and large order—not to mention strike votes and ratification of 125,000 agreements. It would also be unnecessary, if standards were established by law for elections and for members' rights and if provision was made for either self-enforcement or for approved private arrangements and tribunals. For instance, some unions use the Honest Ballot Association to conduct their elections, and the Upholsterers' Union and the United Automobile Workers have set up private review boards of distinguished citizens, to whom members can appeal against actions of the union administration and whose decisions are final and binding on the union. This leads to the third issue of self-enforcement by the labor movement rather than having the government take over some of the decision-making power and much of the enforcement.

Obviously, self-enforcement by the union movement has certain shortcomings and weaknesses. They exist despite the fact that the new federation, growing out of the merger of AFL-CIO in December 1955, has shown commendable fortitude in adopting six "codes of ethical practices" and in suspending or expelling a number of affiliated unions whose administrations have violated those codes. One of the weaknesses is that the AFL-CIO coverage is incomplete; the independent, unaffiliated unions with some one and a half million members in 1956 cannot be touched by it. Another is that the AFL-CIO has no subpoena power, so that it is unable to require its own affiliates to divulge sworn facts about individual officials. A third is that AFL-CIO's only present remedy or means of punishment to achieve compliance is to suspend or expel the offending affiliate, which really means permitting it to escape the federation's standards.

Some within the AFL-CIO look to that union center to exercise additional influence and power over its affiliates. There has even been an assumption that the AFL-CIO will soon be able, on its own authority, to reach in and suspend or expel officers in affiliated unions. However, the tradition of union autonomy and the insistence of national officers upon no invasion of the sovereign rights of their unions, seem likely to prevent the national unions from granting the AFL-CIO any such authority. Gradually, over a considerable period of time, our union center is likely to accumulate more functions and power, as the LO has done in Sweden since the mid-1930's. But during the next few years, minor revolts against the imposition of even AFL-CIO codes of ethical practice are likely to occur.

Various steps are possible short of government adjudication of member-union disputes and government-conducted elections. For the most part they would involve building on previous developments voluntarily instituted. For instance, by statute some of the principles of the AFL-CIO codes of ethical practice could be made Federal standards with which all unions would have to comply, but with latitude in the means by which compliance is accomplished. The unions themselves or the AFL-CIO might establish public review boards (as the Upholsterers and the UAW have done) to hear and rule on aggrieved members' appeals. Or the method used for jurisdictional disputes in the Taft-Hartley Act might be adopted, under which the NLRB is empowered to determine the dispute unless, within ten days after notice that a charge has been filed, the parties themselves have satisfactorily settled the issue. This provision led the parties, in 1948, to establish a private National Joint Board for settling jurisdictional disputes in building construction.

With respect to elections, each national union could be required by statute to certify that all parts of the union had complied with certain statutory requirements regarding the frequency and methods of balloting. That would place upon national unions the responsibility for enforcement, and would leave to each union the method by which compliance was accomplished.

Some of the abuses uncovered by the McClellan Committee are perhaps better handled by reliance on public opinion following reporting, disclosure, and check on the reports (where necessary) through investigation by a governmental agency. This is particularly true of matters of judgment, such as the need for and proper duration of a receivership over a local union, or possible conflicts of interest on the part of union officials. Abuse of the trustee device by national union presidents would be much less likely or prevalent, with disclosure of the facts, full accounting of stewardship, and periodic review of the case, placing the burden of proof on the union's administration as to why the receivership had not been terminated with full power to elect their own officials restored to the local members.

It should be evident from these examples that individual protections and democratic procedures can be established or preserved without the Federal Government becoming a participant in or official custodian for every national and local union. And no amount of Federal legislation can assure the spirit required for successful operation of union democracy or an attitude of fair play toward differences of opinion.

That brings us to the fourth issue, namely, the amount of government intervention that would threaten to rob unions of their independence and vigor. Organized labor in many other countries has been wholly or partially controlled by the government. In many cases unions are, for all practical purposes, creatures of the state, unable to take positions independent of the current government. Under such circumstances, free collective bargaining is nonexistent, and responsible self-regulation by the unions themselves cannot develop. Their evolution is not self-directed, but steered or stopped by the state.

To those who stress the importance of independent centers of opinion in a democratic society, the trend toward more and more Federal encroachment into union-management relations and into union affairs may seem ominous. The danger of government control is indirect as well as direct. Federal intervention tends to stimulate further centralization within the labor movement, with accompanying loss of vitality at the local level. Moreover, government regulation in the labor field has few logical stopping points; control over one aspect of union affairs or union-management relations is prone to expand to others. Before going far down that road, one may wish to consider carefully not only the possible stopping points but also the implications of the particular legislation for the future evolution of unions in this country.

An Evolutionary Perspective

In formulating public policy for organized labor, one ought to keep his eye on the main currents in the moving stream of union affairs and not be too distracted by the eddies or the scum on the surface. An overall view of the American labor movement from an evolutionary perspective provides a salutary corrective for alarms that arise from particular events or a myopic examination of abuses. Too often, long-run factors are overlooked in a headlong rush to enact some punitive legislation. An advantage of underlying trends is that they work slowly but surely and do not make the details of labor relations ardent issues of partisan politics in national election campaigns. Moreover, study of trends discloses decadent as well as dynamic tendencies and the ways by which "grave problems" ultimately get solved or solve themselves.

An evolutionary perspective is likely to lead to faith not only in the bargaining process but in the long-run influence of public opinion. Indeed, some students of American labor believe that moral suasion and community standards are the only fundamental and lasting remedies for abuses in the labor field. And the more settled and integrated American unionism becomes, the more effective cultural incentives will be. Of course, disclosure of facts is a necessary element in the operation of public opinion.

Trade unionism in this country has come a long way. Today it is so typically American that it mirrors most of the good and bad qualities of our society. Not only is unionism part of the daily lives of eighteen million workers, but its influences extend far beyond them. Society, in turn, has been molding the character of organized labor.

The formative stage of American unionism is now largely completed. The union empires have largely been built. Organized labor in this country has acquired its chief institutional characteristics. Changes, of course, will continue in the institutional life of unions, but mostly within the framework already constructed. They are likely to be part of the general developments in American society and not special union mutations. In many respects, American unionism has been maturing, and the features of institutional middle age should be increasingly evident in the years ahead.

FOOTNOTE REFERENCES

CHAPTER I

1. Hoxie, p. 72.
2. *Ibid.*, p. 99. See also p. 65.
3. Perlman, *A Theory of the Labor Movement*, 1928. For a criticism see Charles Gulick and Melvin Bers, "Insight and Illusion in Perlman's Theory of the Labor Movement," *Industrial and Labor Relations Review*, vi (July 1953), pp. 510-531.
4. George W. Brooks, "Reflections on the Changing Character of American Labor Unions," *Proceedings of the Ninth Annual Meeting of Industrial Relations Research Association, December 28 and 29, 1956*, edited by L. Reed Tripp, 1957, pp. 33-43.
5. The results of much of that study are contained in reports published by the Industrial Relations Section of Princeton University. See, for example, *Wages Under National and Regional Collective Bargaining* (1946), *Constructive Labor Relations* (1948), *Job Modifications under Collective Bargaining* (1950), and *Compulsory Arbitration of Utility Disputes in New Jersey and Pennsylvania* (1951).
6. The details of the English and Swedish study are reported in R. A. Lester, "Reflections on Collective Bargaining in Britain and Sweden," *Industrial and Labor Relations Review*, x (April 1957), pp. 375-401.

CHAPTER II

1. K. M. Thompson, "Human Relations in Collective Bargaining," *Harvard Business Review*, xxxi (March-April 1953), p. 119; W. Ellison Chalmers *et al.*, *Labor-Management Relations in Illini City*, Vol. i, The Case Studies, 1953, pp. 100-101.
2. Richard Centers, "Motivational Aspects of Occupational Stratification," *Journal of Social Psychology*, xxviii (November 1948), pp. 187-218; same author, *The Psychology of Social Classes, A Study in Class Consciousness*, 1949.
3. C. Kerr, F. H. Harbison, J. Dunlop, and C. A. Myers, "The Labour Problem in Economic Development," *International Labour Review*, lxxi (March 1955), p. 13; L. Sayles and G. Strauss, *The Local Union*, 1953, pp. 4 and 15.
4. J. Chernick and M. Berkowitz, "The Guaranteed Wage—The

Economics of Opulence in Collective Bargaining," *The Journal of Business*, xxviii (July 1955), pp. 172-173 and 176.

5. A. Kornhauser, H. L. Sheppard, and A. J. Mayer, *When Labor Votes, A Study of Auto Workers*, 1956, pp. 279 and 281.

6. *Ibid.*, pp. 118 and 272; H. Rosen and R. A. H. Rosen, *The Union Member Speaks*, 1955, p. 47; F. X. Sutton, S. E. Harris, and J. Tobin, *The American Business Creed*, 1956, p. 397.

7. Kornhauser, *op. cit.*, p. 268; Rosen and Rosen, *op. cit.*

8. "Report on Second World Conference of Sociology," *International Social Science Bulletin*, vi, No. 1, 1954, p. 34; C. Kerr, "Industrial Conflict and Its Mediation," *American Journal of Sociology*, lx (November 1954), pp. 231-233.

9. For a further discussion of union economic objectives, see A. M. Ross, *Trade Union Wage Policy*, 1948, Chapters 1 and 2.

CHAPTER III

1. *Political Parties; A Sociological Study of the Oligarchical Tendencies in Modern Democracy*, 1915. Some of the factors promoting central control in unions are discussed by S. Lipset, "The Political Process in Trade Unions: A Theoretical Statement" in M. Berger, T. Abel, and C. H. Page (editors), *Freedom and Control in Modern Society*, 1954, pp. 82-122.

2. See Leonard Sayles and George Strauss, *The Local Union: Its Place in the Industrial Plant*, 1951, pp. 24 and 42.

3. The change in the characteristics of union leaders is discussed by Solomon Barkin in "Human Relations in the Trade Unions," published in C. M. Arensberg *et al.* (editors), *Research in Industrial Human Relations*, 1957, pp. 202-204.

4. The relatively new Teamsters, Machinists, and AFL-CIO headquarters in Washington are examples.

5. An example of the belligerent union leader grown to labor maturity is given in *Business Week*, October 20, 1956, p. 98.

6. Professor Sumner H. Slichter has discussed the economic basis of this development in American society in "The Growth of Moderation," *Atlantic Monthly*, cxcviii (October 1956), pp. 61-64.

7. See, for example, L. F. Urwick, *The Pattern of Management*, 1956, p. 6.

8. *Daily Labor Report*, October 2, 1956, pp. 1-2, and October 8, 1956, p. A6.

9. See Daniel Bell, "Steel's Strangest Strike," *Fortune*, civ (September 1956), p. 125.

CHAPTER IV

1. The contrasting views in these two paragraphs are briefly stated by Arthur Kornhauser in *Industrial Conflict*, 1954, edited by Korn-

hauser, R. Dubin, and A. M. Ross, p. 519. Professor Kornhauser favors the second view, namely, that forces within industry and in society in general fluctuate with no definite trend.

2. Named after Frederick W. Taylor, whose books were published in 1903, 1906, and 1911.

3. Reported most completely in F. J. Roethlisberger and W. V. Dickson, *Management and the Worker*, 1939. See also Elton Mayo, *The Social Problems of an Industrial Society*, 1945.

4. In 1950, Solomon Barkin, research director of the Textile Workers Union of America, contended that only management's tactics had been altered. See "A Trade Unionist Appraises Management Personnel Philosophy," *Harvard Business Review*, xxviii (September 1950), p. 59.

5. Douglass V. Brown and Charles A. Myers conclude that the changes in management's philosophy toward employees during the past two decades are "irreversible, short of world upheaval." See "The Changing Industrial Relations Philosophy of American Management," *Proceedings of the Ninth Annual Meeting of Industrial Relations Research Association*, December 28-30, 1956, p. 90.

6. Brown and Myers believe that a stiffer management attitude in recent years has temporarily marked "a reversal or retardation of the longer-run trends." See *ibid.*, p. 94.

7. Of the 171 companies represented on the directorate of NAM in 1955, a total of 93 had agreements with unions affiliated with AFL-CIO. Of those 93 agreements, 71 were in states permitting union-security clauses and 59 of them (83 per cent) contained such provisions. See *Collective Bargaining Report*, Vol. 1, No. 6, June 1956.

8. See Slichter, "The Growth of Moderation," *Atlantic Monthly*, cxlviii (October 1956), pp. 61-64.

9. For a discussion of the cultural climate see, for example, William H. Whyte, Jr., *The Organization Man*, 1956.

10. For data on union participation in community services see articles by Leo Perlis and Matthew Woll in J. B. S. Hardman and M. F. Neufeld (editors), *The House of Labor*, 1951, pp. 333-344, and "Your Community—Labor's New Frontier," *Nation's Business*, xliv (October 1956), pp. 29-31, 84-85.

11. See Rosen and Rosen, *The Union Member Speaks*, 1955, p. 108.

CHAPTER V

1. Jack Barbash states: "Leadership which has rationalized unionism as part of a broader program of social reform has been less prone to engage in dishonest practices." *American Economic Review*, xxxiii (December 1943), p. 876.

2. See, for example, Henry Simons, "Some Reflections on Syndical-

ism," *Journal of Political Economy*, LII (March 1944), pp. 1-25; J. R. Hicks, *The Theory of Wages*, 1932, p. 154; William Fellner, "Prices and Wages under Bilateral Monopoly," *Quarterly Journal of Economics*, LXI (August 1947), pp. 503-532; and C. E. Lindblom, *Unions and Capitalism*, 1949. John T. Dunlop speculates on the economic variable that unions may seek to maximize in his *Wage Determination under Trade Unions*, 1944.

3. See Lloyd G. Reynolds, "Wage Bargaining, Price Changes, and Employment," *Proceedings of the First Annual Meeting of Industrial Relations Research Association*, December 29-30, 1948, p. 44; and Clark Kerr, "Discussion," *ibid.*, p. 51. See also Lloyd G. Reynolds, *The Evolution of Wage Structure*, 1956, p. 190.

4. See Paul Douglas, *Real Wages in the United States*, 1890-1926, 1930, Chapter 31; A. Ross and W. Goldner, "Forces Affecting the Interindustry Wage Structure," *Quarterly Journal of Economics*, LXIV (May 1950), pp. 254-281; and Milton Friedman, "Some Comments on the Significance of Labor Unions for Economic Policy" in D. McC. Wright (editor), *The Impact of the Union*, 1951, pp. 204-259. For an opposite view see Sumner H. Slichter, "Do the Wage-Fixing Arrangements in the American Labor Market Have an Inflationary Bias?" *Papers and Proceedings of the 66th Annual Meeting of the American Economic Association, American Economic Review*, XLIV (May 1954), pp. 322-346.

5. Reynolds, *loc. cit.*

6. See Clark Kerr, "Labor's Income Share and the Labor Movement," in G. W. Taylor and F. C. Pierson (editors), *New Concepts in Wage Determination*, 1957, pp. 260-298. The term "sleepy monopoly" was first applied to business enterprise and only later has occasionally been used with reference to unions.

CHAPTER VI

1. See, for example, Robert Michels, *Political Parties*, first published in 1915 and reprinted by the Free Press, 1949, p. 311.

2. See *John Herling's Labor Letter*, September 28, 1957, p. 4 for an analysis of "Why Canada Is Relatively Free from Racketeering." For a good survey of corruption in American unionism by an Englishman see John Hutchinson, "Corruption in American Trade Unions," *The Political Quarterly*, XXVIII (July-September 1957), pp. 214-235.

3. The charge that the mores of the society and the union power structure have been corrupting influences is made by Kermit Eby in "The Glass-Top Desk," *Christianity Today*, I (December 10, 1956), pp. 15-17 ff.

4. Quoted from George A. Graham, *Morality in American Politics*, 1952, p. 301.

5. As reported in the *Congressional Record*, May 29, 1957, pp. 7146-7151.

6. For example, the president of the Meat Cutters and Butcher Workmen reported yearly expenses of $12,400.13 on May 7, 1956 (see *ibid.*), and the records of the Senate Select Committee on Improper Activities in the Labor and Management Field showed that the president of the Bakery and Confectionery Workers' International Union charged the union $39,000 for expenses in 1956 (*Hearings before the Select Committee on Improper Activities in the Labor or Management Field*, 85th Congress, 1st Session, Part 8, June 19, 1957, p. 2944). The Bakers' president claimed that at least $15,000 to $20,000 of the total was charged as "entertainment" for which there were no vouchers in the union files.

7. For a contrast of the appointive and other powers of top union officials in the United States and England, see B. C. Roberts, *Trade Union Government and Administration in Great Britain*, 1956, pp. 262 and 281.

8. Excerpts from his address before the Coal Mining Institute of America were reported in the *Daily Labor Report*, No. 242, December 13, 1956, p. A5.

9. See *Hearings before the Select Committee on Improper Activities in the Labor or Management Field*, Part 8, June 7, 1957, pp. 2687 and 2718-2721.

10. In March 1957, the Committee was receiving some 100 letters a day, and had a total of 20,000, over four-fifths from union members. The material in this paragraph is based on "Why Union Men Are Complaining," *U.S. News and World Report*, March 29, 1957, pp. 29-33, and a United Press dispatch in the *Newark Sunday News*, April 7, 1957, p. 2.

CHAPTER VII

1. For a discussion of the organizational set-up, bargaining patterns and practices, and governmental intervention in industrial relations in both countries, see the author's article, "Reflections on Collective Bargaining in Britain and Sweden," *Industrial and Labor Relations Review*, x (April 1957), pp. 375-401.

The conclusions in this chapter rest in good part on a study the author made in 1956 in England and Sweden, the results of which are reported in the above article.

2. Professor B. C. Roberts (in his book on *Trade Union Government and Administration in Great Britain*, 1956, p. 467) comments: "It is significant that the developments in British trade unionism have produced a new type of trade union leader who, towards the end of his career looks, not for a seat in the House of Commons, but for

an opportunity of giving further service as an administrator on a public board of some kind." For a remark on the TUC convention of a non-sectional view see *ibid.*, p. 441.

3. *Ibid.*, pp. 141 and 276.

4. One exception, for instance, is the Union of Post Office Workers, which has three to four times as many candidates for the executive council as there are council posts, which has stirring floor debates on issues, and which not infrequently finds a majority of the delegates opposing the recommendations of the executive council.

5. For a discussion of "unofficial strikes" see Lester, *op. cit.*, p. 387 and the reference there to Knowles' book on *Strikes*. The data on the rise of actual earnings above rates negotiated in national agreements are from H. A. Turner, "Wages: Industry Rates, Workplace Rates and the Wage-Drift," *The Manchester School of Economic and Social Studies,* xxiv (May 1956), pp. 95-123.

6. Of course, it is to be expected that, under nationally fixed piece rates, workers' earnings would rise more than the negotiated increases because over a period of time workers would tend to get the advantage of minor improvements in production techniques that occur in particular shops. That factor alone, however, is not sufficient to explain the one-fifth increase.

7. The statements with respect to strike statistics are based on K. G. J. C. Knowles, *Strikes, A Study in Industrial Conflict,* 1952, pp. 27 and 310, adjusted for labor-force increases; and A. M. Ross and D. Irwin, "Strike Experience in Five Countries, 1927-47: An Interpretation," *Industrial and Labor Relations Review,* iv (April 1951), p. 329, and brought up to date.

8. These two paragraphs are based primarily on an interview the writer had April 19, 1956 with August Linberg, who was president of LO from 1936 to 1946.

9. For a discussion of wage developments in Sweden from 1939 to 1956 see Gösta Rehn, "Swedish Wages and Wages Policies," *Annals of the American Academy of Political and Social Science,* cccx (March 1957), pp. 99-108.

10. See Jorgen Westerstahl, *Svensk Fackforenigsrorelse,* 1945.

11. Interview the author had with Arne Geijer, then president of the Metal Workers Union, on April 19, 1956.

12. Rehn, *op. cit.,* Table 1, p. 100.

13. See *Trade Unions and Full Employment,* Swedish Trade Union Federation (English edition, 1953), and also Rehn, *op. cit.,* pp. 106-108.

CHAPTER VIII

1. Matthew Josephson, *Sidney Hillman: Statesman of American Labor,* 1952, pp. 137-139 and 268.

2. A good official history of the Amalgamated is contained in Hyman H. Bookbinder and Associates, *To Promote the General Welfare: The Story of the Amalgamated*, 1950. *The General Executive Board Report and Proceedings of the Twentieth Biennial Convention of the Amalgamated*, May 21-25, 1956 contains up-to-date material on the union's activities as well as a "Special Commemorative Section" on the "Hillman Heritage."

3. See "UAW's Quiet Transformation," *Business Week*, April 20, 1957, p. 154.

4. See, for instance, Irving Howe and B. J. Widdick, *The UAW and Walter Reuther*, 1949, especially Chapter 11.

5. A popular summary of the UAW's history is contained in the 20th Anniversary Edition of *Ammunition* (June 1956), pp. 2-48.

6. Much of this section on the Carpenters rests on Robert A. Christie, *Empire in Wood: A History of the Carpenters' Union*, 1956.

7. For this section on the Teamsters use has been made of Robert D. Leiter, *The Teamsters Union: A Study of Its Economic Impact*, 1957; Chapter 7 on "The Future of the Teamsters' Union" in Philip Taft, *The Structure and Government of Labor Unions*, 1954; and articles by Paul Jacobs on "The World of Jimmy Hoffa," in *The Reporter*, XVI (January 24, 1957), pp. 13-18 and (February 7, 1957), pp. 10-17.

8. Robert D. Leiter, "Structure and Policy in the Teamsters Union," *Monthly Labor Review*, LXXX (October 1957), p. 1185.

9. Leiter, *The Teamsters Union*, p. 113.

10. This section draws heavily from B. Karsh and J. London, "The Coal Miners; A Study of Union Control," *Quarterly Journal of Economics*, LXVIII (August 1954), pp. 415-436, and the Convention Proceedings and Constitution of the union.

11. *Proceedings of the Thirty-fourth Convention of the United Mine Workers of America*, 1936, Vol. I, pp. 122 and 130.

12. Karsh and London, *op. cit.*, pp. 434-435.

13. *Proceedings of the Forty-second Consecutive Constitutional Convention of the United Mine Workers of America*, 1956, Vol. I, p. 332.

14. *Ibid.*, pp. 437-438.

15. *Ibid.*, p. 309.

CHAPTER IX

1. The organizational labor force includes all wage and salary employees. See the calculations in Daniel Bell, "Discussion of Union Growth," *Proceedings of the Seventh Annual Meeting of the Industrial Relations Research Association*, December 28-30, 1954, edited by L. Reed Trip, 1955, p. 233. See also H. P. Cohany, "Membership of American Trade Unions, 1956," *Monthly Labor Review*, CXXX (October 1957), pp. 1205-1206.

2. See J. I. Griffin, *Strikes: A Study in Quantitative Economics*, 1939, especially Chapters 3, 5, and 10.

3. See, for example, the comments of Woodrow L. Ginsburg in *Proceedings of the Ninth Annual Meeting of the Industrial Relations Research Association*, December 28 and 29, 1956, edited by L. R. Tripp, 1957, pp. 44-46.

CHAPTER X

1. For some supporting illustrations see the work of the Committee for Economic Development or A. A. Berle's *The 20th Century Capitalist Revolution*, 1954.

2. Dale Yoder and Roberta J. Nelson, "Salaries and Staffing Ratios in Industrial Relations, 1957," *Personnel*, xxxiii (July 1957), p. 18. Similar annual studies covering the preceding nine years show a fairly stable ratio for the decade, with the large firms having fewer staff per 100 employees.

3. Based on an estimate of 60,000 full-time employees of American unions. In 1951, Lubell used a figure of 55,000 (See Samuel Lubell, *The Future of American Politics*, 1951, p. 182).

4. See *The Organization Man*, 1956.

5. Helen Baker and Robert R. France, *Centralization and Decentralization in Industrial Relations*, 1954, pp. 66-69 and 196.

6. *Ibid.*, pp. 195 and 201.

7. Robert R. France, *Union Decisions in Collective Bargaining*, 1955. The remarks in this paragraph are based primarily on conclusions expressed by France, pp. 15, 25-26, and 44-48.

8. Popularly this program is known as "Boulwareism," after Lemuel Boulware, who has been vice president in charge of industrial relations at G. E.

9. Douglass V. Brown and Charles A. Myers seem to express a contrary view in their article on "The Changing Industrial Relations Philosophy of American Management," *Proceedings of Ninth Annual Meeting of Industrial Relations Association*, December 28 and 29, 1956, edited by L. Reed Tripp, 1957, p. 94. They state: "In the last few years, there seems to us to have been a trend in the direction of a stiffer attitude toward unions on the part of management. . . . For the moment, it is enough to record our impression that, to a significant degree, a stiffening of attitudes and actions has occurred in recent years, momentarily at least marking a reversal or retardation of the longer-run trends."

10. H. Rosen and R. A. H. Rosen in their article on "The Union Business Agent Looks at Collective Bargaining" (*Personnel*, xxxiii, May 1957, pp. 540-542) emphasize the desire of the twenty-one building agents they studied to achieve respect and a good relationship with the company.

11. The larger role that these factors have come to play in bargaining in the automobile industry is mentioned by John S. Bugas in a talk entitled "Industrial Relations—1975," given April 24, 1957 and published by the Ford Motor Company (see p. 17).

12. For a statement of that position see the chapter on industrial disputes in J. R. Hicks, *Theory of Wages*, 1932.

CHAPTER XI

1. Simons, "Some Reflections on Syndicalism," *Journal of Political Economy*, LII (March 1944), p. 8.

2. Dunlop, *Wage Determination under Trade Unions*, 1944, pp. 39, 44, and 119.

3. Perlman, *A Theory of the Labor Movement*, 1928.

4. Ross, *Trade Union Wage Policy*, 1948, p. 27.

5. See "An Analysis of Union Models as Illustrated by French Enterprise" in *The Theory of Wage Determination*, Proceedings of a Conference held by the International Economic Association, John T. Dunlop (editor), 1957, especially pp. 144-147.

6. Paul H. Douglas, *Real Wages in the United States*, 1930, p. 562; and Arthur M. Ross and William Goldner, "Forces Affecting the Interindustry Wage Structure," *Quarterly Journal of Economics*, LXIV (May 1950), pp. 267-269. Both of these studies can be criticized from a technical viewpoint but the general conclusion appears to be a valid one.

7. See H. A. Turner, "Wages: Industry Rates, Workplace Rates and the Wage-Drift," *The Manchester School of Economic and Social Studies*, XXIV (May 1956), pp. 95-123.

8. See Gösta Rehn, "Swedish Wages and Wages Policies," *Annals of the American Academy of Political and Social Science*, CCCX (March 1957), Table I, p. 100.

9. See J. K. Galbraith, "Market Structure and Stabilization Policy," *Review of Economics and Statistics*, XXXIX (May 1957), pp. 124-133, and the testimony of Gardiner C. Means on *Administered Prices: Hearings before the Senate Subcommittee on Antitrust and Monopoly of the Committee of the Judiciary Pursuant to S.Res. 57*, 85th Congress, 1st Session, Part I, Washington, 1957, pp. 74-125.

10. Estimates by Melvin Rothbaum in *New Concepts in Wage Determination*, 1957, edited by G. W. Taylor and F. C. Pierson, p. 316. Mr. Rothbaum cautions that his estimates are only "rough" ones, based on a "rather limited sample of companies."

11. Special Report on "How Expensive Are 'Fringe Benefits'?" in *U.S. News and World Report*, XLI (October 12, 1956), pp. 97-100.

12. That is the view expressed, for example, in Lloyd G. Reynolds and Cynthia Taft, *Evolution of the Wage Structure*, 1956, p. 65.

13. Allan I. Mendelsohn, "Fringe Benefits and Our Industrial Society," *Labor Law Journal*, vii (June 1956), pp. 325-328 and 379-384.

14. *Ibid.*, p. 383.

15. *Review and Reflection*, 1953, p. 5.

16. Harry Bennett, *We Never Called Him Henry*, 1951, pp. 108-109.

17. "The Harvest Labor Market in California," *Quarterly Journal of Economics*, lxv (November 1951), pp. 463-491.

18. The author has more fully discussed the development and implications of the welfare concept of employment in a Sidney Hillman lecture entitled, "The Revolution in Industrial Employment," delivered at the University of Wisconsin on February 12, 1958 and to be published in the June 1958 issue of the *Labor Law Journal*.

19. For figures on benefit-plan coverage see Joseph Zisman, "Private Employee-Benefit Plans Today," *Social Security Bulletin*, xx (January 1957), pp. 8-21, especially p. 9.

CHAPTER XII

1. See Herbert Parnes, *Union Strike Votes: Current Practice and Proposed Controls*, 1956, pp. 14-16 and 90.

2. Sumner H. Slichter, "The Taft-Hartley Act," *Quarterly Journal of Economics*, lxiii (February 1949), pp. 2 and 30.

3. See *Report to Governor Robert B. Meyner by the Governor's Committee on Legislation Relating to Public Utility Labor Disputes*, Trenton, September 9, 1954, especially pp. 10 and 20.

INDEX

Date Due

MAY 2 2 '67			
JUL 2 1 '81			
SEP 2 7 '61			
OCT 2 2 '77			
MAR 4 '80 FEB 15 '80			
OCT 2 6 1982			
OCT 2 8 1982			
NOV 1 3 '84 NOV 1 '84			
MAY 9 '90			
	PRINTED	IN U. S. A.